# THE [illegible]
# OF H[illegible]DU GODS
# AND RITUALS



Minal - Jayu
With Bliss
Daksha - Yeshwant
July 05

**A. PARTHASARATHY**

First Edition 1983
Second Edition 1985
Third Edition 1989
Fourth Edition 1994
Fifth Edition 2000
Sixth Edition 2001



ISBN No. 81-87111-54-2

Published by
Vedanta Life Institute,
1A, Landsend,
Dongarsi Road, Malabar Hill,
Mumbai 400 006 India
Website: www.vedanta-edu.org

Printed by
Arun Mehta
Vakil & Sons Pvt. Ltd.
Industry Manor,
Appasaheb Marathe Marg,
Worli, Mumbai 400 025 India

# A NOTE ON TRANSLITERATION AND PRONUNCIATION

Saṁskṛtam is transliterated in the English alphabet according to the scheme adopted by the International Congress of Orientalists at Athens in 1912 and, since then, generally acknowledged and accepted universally. The key of this scheme is as follows :

| | | |
|---|---|---|
| अ | a | (but) |
| आ | ā | (ma) |
| इ | i | (it) |
| ई | ī | (beet) |
| उ | u | (put) |
| ऊ | ū | (pool) |
| ऋ | ṛ | * (rhythm) |
| ए | e | (play) |
| ऐ | ai | (high) |
| ओ | o | (toe) |
| औ | au | (loud) |
| ं | ṁ | – Anusvāra (nasalization of preceding vowel) written like the dot above अ in अंश: |
| : | ḥ | – Visarga (aspiration of preceding vowel) written like the two dots after श in अंश: |

| | | | |
|---|---|---|---|
| क | k | (skate) | |
| ख | kh | * (blockhead) | |
| ग | g | (gate) | |
| घ | gh | * (loghut) | |
| ङ | ṅ | (sing) | |
| च | c | (chunk) | |
| छ | ch | * (catch him) | |
| ज | j | (john) | |
| झ | jh | * (hedgehog) | |
| ञ | ñ | (bunch) | |
| ट | ṭ | * (start) | |
| ठ | ṭh | * (anthill) | |
| ड | ḍ | * (dart) | |
| ढ | ḍh | * (godhead) | tongue on upper palate |
| ण | ṇ | * (under) | tongue on upper palate |
| त | t | * (thirsty) | tongue on upper palate |
| थ | th | * (therapy) | tongue on upper palate |
| द | d | * (the) | tongue on upper palate |
| ध | dh | * (godhead) | tongue on upper teeth |
| न | n | (numb) | tongue on upper teeth |
| प | p | (spin) | tongue on upper teeth |
| फ | ph | * (loophole) | tongue on upper teeth |
| ब | b | (bin) | tongue on upper teeth |
| भ | bh | * (abhor) | |
| म | m | (much) | |
| य | y | (young) | |
| र | r | (drama) | |
| ल | l | (luck) | |
| व | v | (in bctwccn wilc and vile) | |
| श | ś | * (shove) | |
| ष | ṣ | * (bushell) | |
| स | s | (so) | |
| ह | h | (hum) | |

* There are no exact English equivalents for the letters listed with an asterisk.

# CONTENTS

# Introduction

THE HINDU scriptures are a unique blend of the subtle philosophy of Vedānta on one hand and gross, fetishist worship on the other. Hinduism appears a strange amalgam of the highest classical literature with gods and goddesses, rituals and festivals, ceremonies and celebrations. The Hindus themselves are confused and confounded by this mixture. The Vedas, the very source of Hinduism, authoritatively proclaim that the Reality is one and one alone. Why then do the Hindus fall into manifold denominations and follow a variety of conflicting spiritual practices? Why so many gods? So many divisions? Sects, creeds and castes? Why then does not Hinduism concentrate on one god, one ritual and one practice like other religions? Such questions have baffled even intellectuals from time immemorial.

The Hindus are not polytheistic. Hinduism speaks of one God that is the supreme Self in all, *Ātman, Brahman.* The different gods and goddesses of the Hindu pantheon are mere representatives of the powers and functions of the one supreme God in the manifested world. There is a general misunderstanding that the Hindu worships innumerable gods and goddesses. The different forms of worship, the number of superstitions and misleading spiritual practices have all contributed to the wrong impression that the Hindus are polytheistic. This is far from the truth. In fact, the Hindu worships one God be it directly as *Brahman* or through manifested representations and expressions.

The Hindu religion is ingeniously designed to treat all types of disorders of the mind. The human mind is most complex. It suffers from multifold diseases. Religion is meant to cure these diseases and regain the spiritual health of individuals. Each individual has to be treated separately according to his disease. There cannot be one doctor, one medicine, one cure for all diseases. Hinduism is like a hospital with its many wards, sections and divisions. Each of them has a distinct purpose to attend to particular needs of a particular disease. They are taken care of by specialists in different departments. All of them put together cater to all types of ailments of all sorts of people so that every one of them can come out of the hospital as a healthy person. So too does Hinduism have different treatments for different types of individuals to make them whole and realise their supreme Godhead.

The mind of man is in a chaotic state because of his *vāsanās,* desires. As long as there are desires within, the mind helplessly runs in all directions seeking fulfilment of its desires. Consequently it is agitated. An agitated mind cannot concentrate. It is unfit for contemplation and meditation which alone lead him to the eternal bliss of Self-realisation. Religion is meant to help man to withdraw his mind from its preoccupation with the world at large and converge it to the single-pointed thought of the Self within. When the mind is brought to single-pointedness it can be directed towards meditation and realisation of the supreme Godhead. Without practising spiritual courses according to one's own constitution, there can be no progress towards meditation and the bliss of realisation.

One cannot stop the mind from its ramblings as long as it possesses desires. To circumvent this great hurdle Hinduism has thoughtfully brought in gods and goddesses, rituals and festivals, ceremonies and celebrations. The master plan of the Hindu sages is to divinise everything in this world since man's attention has always been upon the world. The plan has been drawn logically, scientifically, practically. By this plan the mind is reminded of the Supreme even as it is engaged in the desired objects of the world. For instance, Hinduism has personified wealth and riches in the form of the goddess Lakṣmī. So a man who runs after material wealth is made to remember the goddess in all his transactions. Thus a touch of divinity is lent to his material pursuits. Another man may pursue knowledge. Knowledge is personified as the goddess Sarasvatī. So his mind is also drawn to the higher even though he is engaged in the pursuit of wordly knowledge. Thus there are numerous gods covering the entire sphere of human activities.

The life of a Hindu is a series of prayer and worship. Everything is divinised from the cradle to the grave. There is a ritual associated with every aspect of the Hindu life. The entire passage from birth to death is nothing but a series of rituals and ceremonies, prayer and worship. The idea is to remind his dissipating mind constantly of the purpose of his existence in the world. That is to unfold his Self, to realise his Godhood.

The plan of Hinduism is to help the seekers reach the goal of religion. Religion is derived from the Latin terms *re* and *ligare*. *Re* means back, again, *ligare* means to bind, to unite. Etymologically, religion means "that which binds one back to the origin". The origin of man is his real Self. Religion helps man discover his real Self, his supreme Self, to draw out the divinity in man. Hinduism deals with the process of this union most systematically and scientifically.

These pages cannot do justice to the master plan of the Hindu sages. The greatness of the plan is in its scientific approach and its practicality. It is designed to serve as a friend and benefactor of the childish mind. It helps to pull the mind away constantly from its indulgence in the lower fields of sensuality and fix it on the higher thought of the realisation of the Supreme.

India has always been accepted as a great spiritual country in the world. Hinduism has survived the ravages of time and changing environment. It has withstood the influences of many organised and rich religious institutions. The genius of the *ṛṣis* sages preserved the spiritual culture by keeping the truths and tradition alive among the people as a whole and not confining them to a few erudite scholars. The scholars were given the highest philosophical and religious truths directly through Vedānta — the Upaniṣads, the Bhagavad Gītā and the Brahmasūtras. But these truths were beyond the grasp of the common man. Hence they have been presented in a veiled form through Purāṇic stories, rituals and symbols. The dilution of the supreme wisdom with such stories and illustrations proved more assimilable to the ordinary man. The great truths of the Vedas were thus handed down from generation to generation with their pristine glory.

The Purāṇas contain innumerable stories of gods and goddesses. Many of them are exaggerated narrations bordering on absurdity. The very absurdity of these stories is meant to show that they are not to be taken literally but to be delved into deeper to recognise their allegorical significance. The Purāṇas are so popular in India not only among the illiterate masses but also the intelligentsia. Almost the entire Hindu population treats the Purāṇas with utmost devotion and derive spiritual sustenance from them. The Hindu is deeply aware of the allegorical reference to the supreme Truth in the seemingly absurd stories. The intelligentsia maintains an intuitive perception of the Reality hidden behind the superficial absurdities. But a good many have also taken these narrations literally resulting in superstitions and perversions of truths.

The Hindu philosophical and spiritual truths conveyed through the Upaniṣads and Purāṇic literature have also been ingeniously presented to the masses in the form of symbols. A symbol is a known idol representing the unknown ideal. The art of god-symbolism helps both the literate and the illiterate Hindus. The illiterate derive at least some idea of the supreme Truth through the symbols which help them to maintain their ancient culture and heritage. As for the literate the understanding of the inner significance of the symbols establishes a greater conviction of the Truth that they represent. Symbolism plays an important role in life. Even language which man uses for communicating ideas is symbolic in character. The art of symbolism is not peculiar to Hinduism. Religious and philosophical ideas have been expressed through symbols in other religions as well. It has been an age-old practice.

But no other religion has ever developed this art to the extent Hinduism has done. Hinduism has perfected this art. Unfortunately, this art has not been studied at all by the modern generation with the result that the Hindu symbols have been shorn of their philosophical and religious significances and reduced to mere superstition. Thus Hindus have grown to accept them blindly or reject them as meaningless superstitious beliefs. Hence the need today is to revive this great art and educate the world with the knowledge concerning the symbolic character which gives the deep inner meaning of the different forms of Hindu worship.

This book is meant to initiate the reader into learning this art. It is by no means exhaustive. A few examples of the more popular deities, rituals and ceremonies have been taken and their philosophical significance explained. It should give the reader an insight into the treasures of Hindu thought and unearth the deep truths represented by the symbols.

*A. Parthasarathy*

1A Landsend, Dongarsi Road,
Malabar Hill, Mumbai 400 006
INDIA

# PART I
## Hindu Gods and Goddesses

# Gaṇeśa

GAṆAḤ in Sanskṛit means 'multitude'. *Īśa* means 'Lord'. Gaṇeśa therefore literally means the 'Lord of all beings'. Gaṇeśa is the first son of Lord Śiva. Śiva represents the supreme Reality. The son of Śiva symbolises one who has realised the Reality. One who has discovered the Godhood in him. Such a man is said to be the Lord of all beings.

Gaṇeśa is known by other names as well. Gaṇapati, Gajānana, Vināyaka, Vighneśvara. Gaṇapati has the same literal meaning as Gaṇésa. Gajānana means 'elephant-faced'. *Gaja* = elephant, *ānana* = face. Vināyaka means the supreme leader, literally one who has no leader himself. Vighneśvara is the Lord of all obstacles, worshipped in the initiation of Hindu rituals and ceremonies. As his name suggests Vighneśvara removes all obstacles, overcomes all challenges of life. There is a belief that no undertaking will meet with failure if the grace of Vighneśvara is invoked.

In Hindu mythological literature Gaṇeśa is described as having a human form with an elephant's head. One of the tusks is broken. He has a conspicuously large stomach. He sits with one leg folded in. At his feet a variety of food is spread. A rat sits near the food and looks up at him as if it were asking him for sanction to eat the food. This mystical form of Lord Gaṇeśa represents not only the supreme state of human perfection but the practical path to reach that

state. The details of his description suggest deep philosophical significance which can guide you to reach that ultimate state.

The first step of spiritual education is *śravaṇa* which means listening to the eternal truths of Vedānta. The second step is *manana* which is independent reflection upon those truths. The large ears and head of Gaṇeśa indicate that he had gained previous wisdom through *śravaṇa* and *manana*. An elephant's head on a human body in Gaṇeśa is meant to represent supreme wisdom.

The trunk which springs from his head represents the intellect, the faculty of discrimination which necessarily arises out of wisdom.

Intellect is the discriminating faculty, the discerning ability or the judging capacity in man. Man's intellect is of two distinct types, namely the gross and the subtle. Gross intellect is that aspect of his discrimination which is applicable to the realm of the terrestrial world, that part of the intellect which distinguishes between the pairs of opposites existing in this world, distinguishes between day and night, black and white, joy and sorrow etc. Subtle intellect is the other aspect of his discrimination which distinguishes between the infinite and the finite, the real and the unreal, the transcendental and the terrestrial. A man of realisation like Gaṇeśa is one who has fully developed both his gross and subtle intellects. He has perfect understanding and knowledge of the terrestrial as well as the transcendental.

The trunk of an elephant has the unique capacity of performing both gross and subtle activities. A trunk can uproot a tree. It can pick up a needle from the ground. One rarely finds gross and subtle operations being performed by a single instrument. A spanner which is used for fitting a locomotive is useless for repairing a wrist-watch. The elephant's trunk is an exception to this rule. It serves both ways. So does Gaṇeśa's intellect penetrate the realms of the material and spiritual worlds. That is the state which man must aspire to reach.

A Man-of-Perfection is thus rooted in the supreme wisdom. He is not victimised by *rāga-dveṣa,* likes-dislikes. He is not swayed by agreeable and disagreeable circumstances, pleasant and unpleasant happenings, good and bad environment. In other words, he is not victimised by the pairs of opposites existing in this world. Heat and cold, joy and sorrow, honour and dishonour do not affect him, influence him or harass him. He has transcended the limitations of opposites in the world. He is *dvandva atīta,* beyond opposites. This idea is well represented in Gaṇeśa having two tusks one of which is broken. The common man is tossed between pairs of opposites. Represented by Gaṇeśa's tusks. He should endeavour to overcome the influence of the pairs of opposites in him. Man ought not to act merely by his likes and dislikes; these are his worst enemies which he must control and conquer. When he has completely mastered the influence of these pairs of opposites in him, he becomes a Gaṇeśa.

Gaṇeśa's large belly is meant to convey that a Man-of-Perfection can consume and digest whatever experiences he undergoes. Heat or cold, war or peace, birth or death and other such trials and tribulations do not toss him up and down. He maintains an unaffected grace in and through all these fluctuations of the world. Figuratively, he is represented as being able to stomach and digest all types of experiences.

In Hindu mythology, Kubera, the god of wealth offered a dinner to Gaṇeśa in his palace. Gaṇeśa ate all the food that was prepared for the entire gathering of guests. Thereafter still dissatisfied, he started eating the festive decorations that were used for the occasion. At this juncture his father Lord Śiva approached him and offered him a handful of roasted rice. Gaṇeśa consumed the roasted rice and his hunger was satisfied immediately. This story is a directive to mankind that man can never be satisfied with the joys provided by the world of objects represented by Kubera's feast. Material pursuits can never give peace, contentment or happiness to mankind. The only way to attain absolute fulfilment or peace is by consuming your own *vāsanās,* unmanifest desires in you. The destruction of *vāsanās* is represented by the consumption of roasted rice. When rice is roasted it loses its capacity to germinate. The consumption of roasted rice indicates the destruction of *vāsanās,* desires in you. Thereafter you remain in a state of absolute peace and bliss.

Gaṇeśa sits with one leg folded up and the other leg resting on the ground. The leg on the ground indicates that one aspect of his personality is dealing with the world while the other is ever-rooted in single-pointed concentration upon the supreme Reality. Such a man lives in the world like anyone else, but his concentration and meditation are ever-rooted in the *Ātman* within himself. This idea is symbolised in the above posture.

At the feet of Lord Gaṇeśa is spread an abundance of food. Food represents material wealth, power and prosperity. When a man follows the high principles of living indicated above he achieves these material gains. He has them always at his command though he has an attitude of indifference towards them.

Beside the food is a tiny rat looking up towards Gaṇeśa. The rat does not touch the food but waits for the master's sanction as it were for consuming it. The rat represents desire. A rat has a small mouth and tiny sharp teeth. But it is the greediest of all animals. Its greed and acquisitiveness are so great that it steals more than it can eat and hoards more than it can remember, often abandoning burrows full of hoarded grains through forgetfulness. This predominant trait in a rat justifies amply its symbolism as desire. One little desire entering man's mind can destroy all his material and spiritual wealth earned for many long years. The rat looking up therefore denotes that the desires in a perfect man are absolutely under control. The activities of such a man are motivated by his clear discrimination and judgement rather than by an emotional craving to enjoy the variety of sense-objects of the world.

There is a belief amongst Hindus that it is inauspicious to see the moon on the Vināyaka Chaturthī day, reckoned to be the birthday of Gaṇeśa. As per a Purāṇic story, the moon saw Gaṇeśa riding on his tiny rat and laughed at the ludicrous scene. For this reason the moon is condemned and people are forbidden to see it on this day.

Gaṇeśa riding on his rat indicates a Man-of-Perfection trying to use his limited body, mind and intellect to convey the illimitable Truth. The body, mind and intellect are finite. They cannot express the infinite *Ātman.* A Man-of-Realisation finds it almost impossible to convey his infinite experience through his finite equipments. Hence the words and deeds of all spiritual masters are peculiar and incomprehensible. The common man's intellect cannot comprehend the Truth. The moon is the presiding deity of the mind. The moon laughing at Gaṇapati riding on the rat indicates the ignorant scoffing at the Man-of-Realisation's attempt to convey the Truth. This attitude of scoffing at spiritual preceptors and precepts is detrimental to humanity. The generations are therefore warned not to laugh or scoff at the spiritual messages. If they do, they meet with degradation and disaster.

Gaṇeśa has four arms. The four arms represent the four inner equipments of the subtle body, namely *manas* mind, *buddhi* intellect, *ahaṅkāra* ego and *citta* conditioned-consciousness. Gaṇeśa represents the pure Consciousness, the *Ātman* which enables these four equipments to function in you.

In one hand he holds an axe and in another a rope. The axe symbolises the destruction of all desires and attachments and their consequent agitations and sorrows.

The rope is meant to pull the seeker out of his wordly entanglements and bind him to the everlasting and enduring bliss of his own Self. In the third hand he holds a *modaka* rice ball. *Modaka* represents the joyous rewards of spiritual seeking. A seeker gains the joy of satisfaction and contentment as he progresses on the path of spiritual evolution. In the fourth hand he holds a *padma* lotus. The lotus represents the supreme Goal of human evolution. By holding the lotus in his hand he draws the attention of all seekers to that supreme State that each one of them can aspire for and reach through proper spiritual practices. He blesses all his devotees to reach the supreme State of Reality.

Thus by indicating to mankind the goal of human evolution and the path to reach the same, Lord Gaṇeśa occupies a place of distinction in the Hindu pantheon. May he give us all the strength and courage to pursue the path which he has led and may we gain that supreme Goal which he has reached.

# Subramaṇya

THE SECOND son of Lord Śiva is Subramaṇya, Subramaṇya is also known as Kārtikeya and Ṣaṇmukha. Subramaṇya holds a spear or javelin, *śakti* in his hand. He rides a peacock. The peacock grips a snake with his feet.

Subramaṇya like other gods is a picture of human perfection. Through symbolism, he indicates ways and means to reach that Perfection.

A normal human being goes through three experiences: waking, dream and deep-sleep states of consciousness. Waking state is the state of consciousness which man experiences when he is awake. The dream is the state of consciousness which he experiences when he is dreaming. The deep-sleep is dreamless sleep when he experiences a realm of nothingness. Beyond these three states is the state of God-consciousness. That is the fourth state, called *turīya.* Man is hardly aware of this state much less does he experience it. Nevertheless, that is man's original and real state, the core of his personality, his essential and infinite being. When you transcend the limitations of the waking, dream and deep-sleep you reach that state. This is the state symbolised by Subramaṇya.

Subramaṇya holds a *śakti* spear in his hand. Most of the Hindu gods wield weapons of destruction. Śiva holds

the trident, *triśūla.* Viṣṇu carries a discus, *cakra.* Rāma carries a bow. These weapons are meant to attack, to destroy *vāsanās,* desires within oneself. It is only by the destruction of *vāsanās,* desires that you attain your divine state. Your *vāsanās,* desires are the impurities covering the Godhead within you. Man minus desires is God. God plus *vāsanās* is man. Holding a spear, Subramaṇya proclaims the destruction of all his *vāsanās.* You too, by destroying your *vāsanās,* can attain your supreme Stature.

The peacock is the vehicle of Subramaṇya. The significant characteristic of a peacock is its vanity. The vanity of the peacock is seen during its continuous dancing with its colourful feathers spread out like a fan. The peacock is blue in colour. This subtly suggests the means the seeker should adopt to attain the state of Subramaṇya.

Man is now absorbed in the material layers of his personality. All his attention and interest are upon his physical body, mind and intellect. Identifying himself with them he imagines himself to be a perceiver-actor at the physical level, a feeler at the mental level and a thinker at the intellectual level. He is proud of his physical, mental and intellectual achievements. He is lost in the mire of perceptions, emotions and thoughts. Thus, he assumes a limited personality. He has no glimpse of the supreme Self within him. He has now to shift his attention and concentration from his body, mind and intellect to the Godhead, *Ātman* within him. The Godhead is his supreme Self within. The essential nature of man is his Godhood and not his physical-mental-intellectual personality. He must now lose the false vanity of his physical-mental-intellectual personality, ego and develop the true 'vanity' of his infinite Being. He must ride on the blue bird representing his infinite Being. Blue colour is associated with infinity. The sky is blue, so is the ocean. He must repeat to himself that he is God — *Aham Brahma Asmi; Aham* = I, *Brahman* = God, *Asmi* = am. He must constantly remember the Truth — I am God. If he practises this, concentrates and meditates upon his real Self, he becomes the *Ātman.* He attains the state of Subramaṇya.

The peacock is the enemy of the serpent. It is seen clutching the serpent with its claws. The serpent is not killed but held in captivity. This symbolises complete control over the ego. The serpent represents the ego. The ego carries the poisonous mind. It is interesting to note that the poison in the fangs of the snake does not kill the snake. It is harmful only when it is directed outside. Similarly, the mind is harmless as long as it is contained within. The moment it is directed outside, used extrovertedly it assumes the vanity of I-ness and my-ness. It becomes poisonous. It generates desires and destroys peace and tranquillity. The infinite *Ātman* becomes the limited individual. But when the ego is held firm and the desires are kept under perfect control, man gains mastery over the mind and reaches perfection.

In the Old Testament, Moses is said to have fallen into this state of slavery. Walking on Mount Sinai, Moses saw a serpent. He trembled at the sight of it. Just then he heard a voice saying, "Hold it, hold that hissing serpent, Moses." It was the voice of God. Moses hesitated. He shuddered at the thought of it. The voice was insistent, "Get hold of it".

Moses took a bold step and held the serpent. Instantly, the serpent turned into a staff. And that staff worked miracles. Moses touched a rock with the staff and fresh water gushed forth from it. When the Israelies were fleeing for safety the Red Sea stood in their way. Moses again used his staff. No sooner did his staff touch the sea than the waters divided and dry land appeared before them. Thus the Israelies passed into safety.

Similarly, Reality seems terrifying. You would keep off from it. You would prefer to indulge in the pleasures of your senses. You do not want to stifle your ego and experience your Godhead. You are afraid to leave the comforts of the known and plunge into the unknown. You are ignorant of the supreme bliss of Godhood. Your ignorance is the cause of your fright. Vedānta, the supreme philosophy of life, offers you knowledge to overcome ignorance, emboldens you to smother your ego and reveal your Self. It seems difficult. The suggestion to annihilate your ego appears frightening. But you must take the plunge fearlessly. Get hold of the ego. Destroy your selfishness. Assert your divinity. Embrace your Godhead within. You will become the monarch of all you survey. All your worries and anxieties vanish instantly. You live in perfect peace and bliss.

Another form of Subramaṇya is Ṣaṇmukha. This form has six faces, *ṣat* means six, *mukha* means face. Ṣaṇmukha is a deity with six faces. It only means that the supreme Self expresses itself in the human being through the five sense organs and mind. The Self within has no expression but when It functions through the sense organs and mind It manifests as a human being.

# Śiva

ŚIVA IS one of the gods of the Trinity. He is said to be the god of destruction. The other two gods are Brahmā, the god of creation and Viṣṇu, the god of maintenance. The three gods represent the three fundamental powers of nature which are manifest in the world viz. creation, destruction and maintenance. These powers exist perpetually. Creation is going on all the time. So is destruction and maintenance. All three powers are manifest at all times. They are inseparable. Creation and destruction are like two sides of a coin. And maintenance is an integral part of the processes of creation and destruction. For example, morning dies to give birth to noon. Noon dies, night is born. In this chain of birth and death, the day is maintained. To indicate that these three processes are one and the same, the three gods are combined in one form of Lord Dattātreya. Lord Dattātreya has the faces of Brahmā, Viṣṇu and Śiva.

Śiva is married to the Goddess Umā. Umā represents *prakṛti* which means perishable matter. Śiva's marriage with Umā signifies that the power of destruction has no meaning without its association with perishable matter. Destruction manifests itself only when there is perishable matter.

Lord Śiva sits in a meditative pose against the white background of the snow-capped Himālayas in Mount

Kailāsa. His posture symbolises perfect inner harmony and poise, experienced by a Man-of-Realisation. He is rooted in God-consciousness. He revels in the bliss of the transcendental Reality. Nothing disturbs him. The vicissitudes of nature, the challenges of life, the trials and tribulations of the terrestrial world do not affect him at all. He maintains perfect serenity, equanimity and tranquillity in all environments and circumstances.

The snow-white background symbolises the absolute purity of mind. When the mind is disturbed, agitated you do not see the divinity in you. Recognising your divine Self is like seeing a reflection in a pool of water. When the water is dirty or disturbed you cannot see your own reflection. Only when the water is clear and steady do you recognise your reflection. Similarly, the divinity in you is lost in a pool of thoughts. If the thoughts are dirty, *tāmasika* or agitated, *rājasika* you miss your divine Self. By spiritual practices you ought to raise your personality, from its *tāmasika* and *rājasika* states to the state of *sattva.* In the *sāttvika* state, when the mind is absolutely pure and steady you recognise your supreme Self. That is the state of Śiva in Kailāsa.

Lord Śiva not only represents the supreme state of perfection in man but in his very pose indicates the way to reach it as well. Śiva has his eyes half-closed, that is neither fully closed nor fully open. It is called *samabhāvīmudrā.* Closing the eyes completely would mean that the individual has shut out the world. He is not at all in this world. Opening the eyes fully would mean that he is totally involved in this world. Half-closed eyes therefore signify that his mind is absorbed in the inner Self while his body is engaged in the outer world. One

aspect of his personality is ever-rooted in God-consciousness while the other is dealing with his wordly duties and responsibilities. He conducts himself in this world like an actor does on the stage. An actor plays various roles but in truth he has nothing to do with them. He retains his real identity throughout the play and merely acts the scenes detachedly. So is the man of Realisation in this world. Ever-rooted in *Ātmic* Consciousness, he goes about in the world like any other man.

The state of meditation shown in Śiva's posture is again symbolic. Meditation is the final gateway to Self-realisation. To attain the state of Godhood you need to meditate. However, in order to meditate successfully you must possess a pure mind. To develop a pure mind you need to work impersonally in this world. The process of self-development first necessitates selfless dedicated actions, *karma*. By such *karma* your ego and egocentric desires fall away. In the process your mind gets purified. Such a man is brought to the state of meditation. Through meditation you realise your supreme Self. All that is suggested in the pose of Lord Śiva sitting in Kailāsa amidst snow-capped mountains.

On the auspicious occasion of Mahāśivarātri, Śiva performs the ecstatic dance of realisation. In the dance pose Śiva is known as Naṭarāja. The dance symbolises the thrill of God-realisation. Beyond the realms of the waking, dream and deep-sleep states of consciousness. Beyond the experiences of the body and its perceptions, the mind and its feelings, the intellect and its thoughts lies the bliss of Godhood. Śiva reaches this state of Godhood and dances with the intoxication of supreme Bliss.

Śiva is said to have a third eye known as *jñāna cakṣu. Jñāna cakṣu* literally means eye of wisdom. The eye whose vision reaches beyond that of the two mortal eyes. The idea of the third eye is not to be taken literally to mean that a third fleshy organ exists in Śiva. It only means that Śiva has a divine vision of Reality. Your vision is confined merely to perceptions, emotions and thoughts but when you transcend the limitations of your body, mind and intellect you gain realisation of your inner Self. That is indicated by the opening of the *jñāna cakṣu.*

A man of Realisation is one who has conquered his ego, is the master of his ego, unlike the wordly people who are victimised by the demands of the ego. In the Hindu scriptures ego is represented as a serpent. The ego serpent harasses you with its venom of desires. Man suffers all his lifetime from the pressure of his own desires. You use your ego to pronounce your limited personality. Consciously or unconsciously you repeat to yourself that you are your body, mind and intellect. You hypnotise yourself to believe "I am the perceiver", "I am the feeler", "I am the thinker". Thus you assume a limited personality of perceiver-feeler-thinker which is pressurised by the demands of the body, mind and intellect. When you change your focus of attention from the body, mind and intellect to the supreme Self within, when your ego takes to the Supreme in you, when you identify yourself with your immortal Self you become the immortal Śiva. When you develop the ego of the supreme Self you become God. The same ego that has degraded you into a limited existence now 'adorns' your personality. This idea is indicated by Śiva coiling the serpent around his neck.

(There is an Indian custom of men wearing a folded cloth around the neck as a decoration.)

Śiva is also known as Gaṅgādhara. Gaṅgādhara literally means the carrier of Gaṅgā (River Ganges). Śiva is said to carry the Ganges in his locks. There is a mythological story describing the descent of the river Ganges from the heavens to earth. The origin of the Ganges is said to be in the heavens, where it is known as *Ākāśa-gaṅgā*. *Ākāśa-gaṅgā* is personified in mythology as a goddess. King Bhagīratha prayed to the goddess to descend from the heavens and bless the people of the earth with her prosperity. The prayer was granted. *Ākāśa-gaṅgā* was willing to come down to earth. The goddess however warned Bhagīratha that the flow of water from the heavens will be so torrential, that the earth would not be able to bear its force. The only person able to receive such torrential flow being Lord Śiva. So Bhagīratha again went into penance and prayer and implored Śiva to bear the flow of descent of the waters. Śiva acceded. He received the waters of the *Ākāśa-gaṅgā* in his locks where they were imprisoned. Śiva retired to the jungles for meditation. But the Gaṅgā did not flow on the earth. The king again implored Śiva, this time to release the waters of the holy Gaṅgā from his locks for the people of the world. As the story goes the Lord granted this prayer as well. The present Gaṅgā is said to be the water flowing out of Śiva's locks.

Strange as the story may sound it has a deep inner significance. Gaṅgā stands for the ultimate Truth, the ultimate Reality, the knowledge of the *Ātman* or Divinity in man. The knowledge of *Ātman* is the state of perfection in man. It is well above the terrestrial realm of experiences. It is symbolically represented as being located above in the heavens. In order to make the divine knowledge available to you a great soul like Bhagīratha is required. Bhagīratha is therefore a sage who brought the divine knowledge to the people of the world. Again, to receive the knowledge of the sages you need to be a man of *tapas* self-control, introvert, contemplative. An indulgent, extroverted man cannot receive spiritual knowledge. The primary qualification needed for the receipt of knowledge is symbolised in the personality of Śiva. Śiva is reputed for his great *tapas*, contemplation and meditation. Such a man alone can describe the great spiritual truths. The truth so received has to be assimilated and ingrained into your life to bring about your spiritual unfoldment. That state is achieved by your independent reflection and meditation which has been indicated by Śiva retiring to the jungles. Having attained spiritual unfoldment, the knowledge of Truth has to be communicated to the people of the world gradually, carefully. The power to understand the higher truth is limited. This idea is again beautifully indicated by the release of the Gaṅgā from Śiva's head in trickles. Thus by gradual and slow education spiritual knowledge is gained in this world. Gaṅgā water stands for spiritual wisdom. Hence a dip in the Gaṅgā is considered sacred. When a pilgrim submerges himself in the sacred river it symbolises his union with the supreme Reality.

Śiva is sometimes shown with a *triśūla* trident in hand. The *triśūla* is a three-pronged weapon which symbolises the destruction of the ego with its three-fold desires of the body, mind and intellect. Śiva with his weapon indicates his victory over his ego and attainment of the state of Perfection.

# Naṭarāja

NAṬARĀJA is Lord Śiva in the dance pose. On Mahāśivarātri day Śiva lays down his *triśūla* trident and performs the ecstatic dance of Naṭarāja. Mahāśivarātri literally means the great night of Śiva. Night or darkness symbolises ignorance—ignorance of the supreme Self. Man is steeped in ignorance. He is enmeshed in the world of plurality. He has no knowledge of the supreme Self within himself. The dance of Naṭarāja on the auspicious night depicts the thrilling experience of Self-realisation, the dawn of the knowledge of the Self, the destruction of spiritual ignorance, the change from the terrestrial to the Transcendental being.

The trident that Śiva carries has three prongs. The three prongs also represent the three *guṇas*, the three thought-textures, viz. *sattva, rajas* and *tamas.* The *sattvaguṇa* is the state of the mind when it is pure, serene and contemplative, *rajoguṇa* when it is passionate and agitated, *tamoguṇa* when it is dull and inactive. These three *guṇas* combined in different degrees of concentration constitute the variety of human beings all over the world. Every human being is composed of the *sāttvika, rājasika* and *tāmasika* thought-patterns enveloping the supreme Self, *Ātman.* When the *guṇas* are eliminated man unfolds his supreme Self and attains Self-realisation. The weapon *triśūla* is meant to destroy the three *guṇas* and realise the *Ātman.*

The laying down of the trident symbolises man's victory over the three *guṇas* and the ecstatic experience of the bliss of the *Ātman.*

The dancing deity has four arms delicately poised. The upper right hand carries a small drum known as the *ḍamaru.* The *ḍamaru* is shaped like an hour-glass. It regulates the rhythm of the dance. The upper left hand makes a half-moon posture with its fingers called *ardha-candra-mudrā.* It bears on its palm a tongue of flame. Naṭarāja is represented as dancing with one foot firm on the prostrate body of a dwarfish demon, *apasmāra puruṣa* and the other foot raised in a well-known posture in Indian classical dance. The ring of flames encompasses the dancing deity. It is known as the *prabhā-maṇḍala.* The lower hands are held in the *abhaya* and the *varada mudrās.*

The dance posture with one leg on the dwarf and the other raised is significant. A Man-of-Perfection lets one aspect of his personality deal with the world below while the other is in single-pointed attunement with his higher Self. The dwarfish demon crushed under the feet of Naṭarāja represents man's ego. The ego is insignificant compared to the *Ātman.* But it has demoniac qualities. It destroys the peace and bliss inherent in man. The ego is conquered and crushed by a Man-of-Perfection. Thereby he regains his supreme Bliss.

Desires, constituting man's ego, represent his lower nature. This lower nature is compared to a serpent in scriptural literature. When desires overpower man he becomes a slave of his own lower nature. It is a disgrace for

him to fall into such a state. The glory of man is to conquer his lower nature, master his desires. That is his dignity and prestige. By coiling a serpent around his neck Naṭarāja proclaims that state of Perfection, of total mastery over desires, senses, ego.

The lower nature of man tempts him with various desires. Consequently man indulges in his senses and gets totally involved in the world. He is bound by attachments to the world. He is afraid to leave the comforts of the known and plunge into the unknown. Naṭarāja symbolises the bold step that a man seeking Perfection takes. The beauty of life is to conquer these desires and realise your Godhead, to revel in the ecstasy of the supreme bliss of Realisation.

Naṭarāja also represents the absolute Reality, *Brahman.* The halo of flames encompassing him signifies the beings, *jīvas* of this world. The primeval source of creation is *Brahman.* When man reaches the state of spiritual Perfection, when he becomes Naṭarāja he merges with that primeval source. Man becomes *Brahman,* the source of all creation. This idea is indicated by the flames issuing forth from Naṭarāja. *Brahman* is the underlying Reality from which the phenomena of creation, destruction and maintenance emerge. This idea is depicted by Naṭarāja holding the drum, *ḍamaru* in one hand and flame in the other. The drum produces sound. Sound is the essence of space, the first of the five elements that constitute all creation. Production of sound therefore indicates the phenomena of creation. The flame on the other hand denotes destruction. The continuous chain of creation and destruction maintains the universe. For example, the seed is destroyed when the tree emerges. The tree perishes giving birth to seed. The egg is no more when the chicken emerges. The chicken dies leaving the egg behind. In this perpetual process of creation and destruction the universe is maintained. This universe arises from *Brahman* from Naṭarāja.

The *abhaya* and *varada mudrās* shown by the lower hands signify the offerings of protection and boons. The allegory of Naṭarāja brings out the dual manifestation of the supreme Reality, *Brahman,* the absolute tranquillity of the pure Self and the dynamic expression of the universe. In one and the same form of Naṭarāja both these aspects are indicated. The Lord maintains a blissful, silent countenance within while he is engaged in his untiring dance. The serenity and utter unconcern in the countenance of Naṭarāja represents the supreme tranquillity of the *Ātman.* In significant contrast, the passionate agility of the swaying limbs of the dance represents the dynamic activity in the world. The effect of the unmanifest and manifest constituting the one Divinity is brought out in this form of Naṭarāja.

Śiva's tresses are long and matted symbolising the continuous *tapas* austerity undertaken by him. However in the triumphant frenzy of his dance of Realisation the tresses loosen and spread out. The suggestion in the loosening of the tresses is that the state of Realisation is trans-*tapas.*

Mythology further relates that in whatever direction Lord Naṭarāja looks with his third eye that part of the world is destroyed. It means that a man of Realisation gains the knowledge of Truth in the light of which the ignorance-created world disappears. With the apprehension of Reality there is no longer the misapprehensions of the pluralistic world. The cosmic dancer shows to mankind the highest ideal that man is to reach and indicates the path to it. He is therefore not to be considered as a mere mythological creation.

# Viṣṇu

VIṢṆU is one of the gods of the Trinity. Viṣṇu represents the power of sustenance. The other two powers manifest in the world, namely creation and destruction are personified as Brahmā and Śiva respectively. Viṣṇu is wedded to Lakṣmī the goddess of wealth. The significance is that sustenance or maintenance involves wealth. In order to maintain anything the maintainer must necessarily possess wealth.

In the *Viṣṇu Purāṇa,* Sage Vyāsa refers to Viṣṇu as the supreme all-pervading Reality, the Reality which is the substratum of the microcosm and macrocosm. The root *'viṣ'* means 'to pervade'. Viṣṇu is the core of the human personality. He is the *Ātman* which manifests Itself through body, mind and intellect as the individual. The same Viṣṇu pervades the entire cosmos as *Brahman.*

Viṣṇu is said to be lying on a great serpent, *Śeṣa* or *Ananta,* in an ocean of milk, *kṣīrābdhi* in heaven, *Vaikuṇṭha.* He is said to be in yogic sleep, *yoganidrā.* The body of the serpent is coiled to form Viṣṇu's bed. The serpent has a thousand heads and its hood is turned inward looking at its own coiled body. Viṣṇu's consort, Lakṣmī, sits at his feet serving him.

Viṣṇu represents the supreme within the human body, mind and intellect. The picture of Viṣṇu lying on the serpent-bed in the milky ocean suggests the means of recognising the *Ātman*, the innermost core of man's personality. The ocean is the mind with its infinite thoughts. The milky ocean stands for the *sāttvika* mind. A *sāttvika* mind is pure and serene. It is the highest quality of the mind. The other two states of the mind are *rājasika* and *tāmasika*. The *rājasika* mind is ever agitated. *Tāmasika* is dull and stupid. When the mind is in the latter two states man gets involved in the mundane world. Only the *sāttvika* mind lifts man to the higher realm of Divinity. In a *sāttvika* mind alone can man recognise his Godhead.

The serpent is the ego with its many desires. In a *sāttvika* mind the ego is turned inward. An extroverted ego loses sight of the Divinity within. When the same ego turns its attention inward, when its concentration is upon the inner Self instead of the outer objects of the world it recognises the supreme Self, *Ātman*. The thousand heads of the serpent turning inward indicate that the thoughts are directed to single-pointed concentration meditation upon the *Ātman*. When man holds his mind thus in deep meditation upon his supreme Self he realises Viṣṇu, the all-pervading Reality.

Viṣṇu is shown to be in yogic sleep—*yoganidrā*. *Yoga* is derived from its root *yuj*, to unite. This indicates his perfect union with the infinite Reality. *Nidrā* means sleep. A man who is totally absorbed in the supreme Self is asleep as it were to the happenings of the terrestrial world, revelling in the infinite bliss of Self-realisation. He is disinterested in the experiences of the finite world.

Goddess Lakṣmī, the consort of Viṣṇu, sits at his feet, serving him. Lakṣmī symbolises the wealth, power and glory of this world. When man seeks the higher Truth and is disinterested in the world the sense-objects seek him. When Viṣṇu is sought, Lakṣmī necessarily follows the seeker. But the trouble in the world today is that people try to seek Lakṣmī directly. The moment man runs after wealth, starts desiring, craving, asking and begging for it, the object of desire leaves him. That is the law.

Viṣṇu is the one eternal, unmanifest Reality. The manifest world of plurality has emerged from the unmanifest Reality. Brahmā, the creator of the world is shown as emerging from the navel of Viṣṇu while he is lying on the serpent-bed. The navel portion represents the psychological centre, *cakra* from where sound originates in the form of *parāvāk,* transcendent speech. This inaudible sound passes through two more stages of development, namely *paśyanti* and *madhyama,* before it becomes audible speech, called *vaikhari.* This audible sound is the quality of space, *ākāśa.* Space is the first of the five elements which constitutes the entire universe. The production of sound therefore symbolises creation. This idea of the manifested world created from the unmanifested Reality is illustrated by Brahmā emerging from the navel of Viṣṇu.

Viṣṇu is known to be blue in colour and clothed in yellow garb. He wears a crown and stands upon a lotus. He has four hands. All these are significant symbols indicating that Viṣṇu is none other than the supreme Self, the changeless Reality around which all the terrestrial changes take place, the imperishable essence in the perishable world.

The blue colour of Viṣṇu indicates His infinite stature. Blue is associated with the infinite since immeasurable entities like the sky or ocean appear blue in colour. Yellow is usually attributed to the earth for two reasons: one, the earth (silica) glows with a yellow fire when introduced in a colourless flame; and two, anything that is buried in the earth for a long period of time gathers a yellowish colour. Viṣṇu, blue in colour and clothed in yellow, therefore, represents the descent of the infinite, immeasurable, transcendental Truth to the terrestrial realm i.e. God in a human form.

When the Infinite expresses through a finite form, there is a manifestation of an individual, *jīva.* The individual comes in contact with and reacts to the world with the help of four subtle instruments in him. They are the four constituents of his subtle body, viẓ *manas* mind, *buddhi* intellect, *ahaṅkāra* ego and *citta* conditioned-consciousness. The four hands of Viṣṇu represent them.

The crown on Viṣṇu's head signifies his supreme sovereignty and lordship over the entire world of plurality. He is the one who maintains and protects all things and beings in the entire universe.

The deity stands upon a lotus. The lotus represents Truth. 'Standing upon the lotus' therefore, means that the ground or substratum which supports a God-man is the *Brahman* i.e. a God-man is ever rooted in the supreme Truth.

In his four hands Viṣṇu holds a *śaṅkha* conch, *cakra* discus, *gada* mace and *padma* lotus. The lotus indicates the final goal of human evolution. By showing the lotus, Viṣṇu invites mankind to reach this goal of perfection by realising his pure Self within. The Lord blows his *śaṅkha* conch, calling the people of the world to lead a pure and noble life so that they may shift their attention and interest from the material world to the supreme Self within. This call is the whispering of the conscience within. The conscience of man tells him to give up sensuous appetites and extrovert living and directs him to the higher life. But man does not heed this sacred voice from within. He continues with his passionate living until he experiences knocks and shocks leading to disappointment and dissatisfaction with life. The mace in the third hand is meant as a warning to draw man's attention to this stern law of nature. If man, despite the growing sense of restlessness and agitations in his bosom, still persists in his sensual indulgences and does not turn towards the spiritual path, he meets with total disaster. The discus is meant to show man this inevitable end that he would reach if he were totally heedless to the warnings of nature.

On the other hand, a seeker who listens to the call from within and follows the spiritual path leading to the Truth, does not experience the knocks of the mace or the destruction of the discus. He lives a life of contentment and bliss until he reaches the sacred abode of Truth and becomes one with Viṣṇu.

Viṣṇu's message conveyed by his four hands is true not only with reference to an individual but to a society, community or a nation as well. As long as people do not heed the sacred advice of the scriptures and take to the spiritual values of life, they meet with sorrow and suffering in life. If this warning also is not heeded and the people continue to live extrovertedly fulfilling merely their sense gratifications, they are bound to meet with disaster. This is what history has been recording from generation to generation as evidenced by the rise and fall of nations and empires.

# Śāstha

ON THE PEAK of Śabarī Hill at the southern tip of the Sahyādrī range stretching southward into Kerala, there is an ancient temple dedicated to Lord Ayyappan who is popularly known as Śabarī Mala Śāstha. This temple can be reached only by foot through the jungle which is infested with wild animals. Thousands of pilgrims reach this shrine trekking through the jungle paths.

Like all of the Hindu deities, Śāstha has a mystical significance. Mysticism is a technique of employing symbols and stories to convey the knowledge of the highest Reality to mankind. It is used by all religions. In the Hindu scriptures this technique has been developed to artistic perfection.

Śāstha is the son of Lord Śiva and Mohinī. Mohinī is the enchanting form of a maiden taken by Lord Viṣṇu. Śāstha is reputed as a very powerful deity. He is considered to be a protector of the weak. He is said to have saved mankind from physical and mental sickness and endowed them with spiritual knowledge.

The scriptures have always represented a constant strife between the gods and the demons. In the Viṣṇu Purāṇa, the gods and demons decided to sink their differences temporarily. They came to a mutual

understanding to make a combined effort to churn the milky ocean and draw the nectar, *amṛtam* from it. They chose the Mandara mountain to serve as the churner and Vāsuki the mighty serpent as a rope for the purpose of churning. The gods and demons stood on opposite sides and started the great churning of the milky ocean.

The churning first produced a deadly poison called *halahala* which started spreading everywhere. Living beings panicked and ran for protection to Lord Śiva. Śiva, in His divine compassion for them, took the poison in his palm and not knowing what to do with it, decided to swallow it himself. When Śiva put it into his mouth and was about to swallow it, his consort Umā clutched his neck and stopped the poison from descending any further. The poison spread through the neck staining it blue. Henceforth he was *Nīlakaṇṭha,* the blue-necked.

The churning went on and several beautiful and powerful things issued from the ocean. They were all distributed and the gods and the demons persisted with their churning until at last the nectar was produced. But as soon as the nectar appeared, the demons snatched and ran away with it.

The gods prayed to Viṣṇu to retrieve their loss. Viṣṇu answered the prayers and agreed to bring back the nectar to them. Meanwhile, the demons quarrelled among themselves. They could not decide as to who should distribute the nectar and the quantity each should get. In such a state of confusion, Lord Viṣṇu appeared in the form of an enchanting maiden, Mohinī. Fascinated by Mohinī the demons stood gazing at her beauty. Having attracted them thus, Mohinī offered to distribute the nectar justly between the gods and the demons. The demons accepted her offer. Viṣṇu made the gods and demons sit in different rows and started the distribution with the gods. By the time the last god had been served the nectar would have run out. One of the demons perceiving this trick left his row and sat among the gods. He got his share and put it in his mouth. Before it could reach his stomach, Mohinī realised her mistake and Viṣṇu's discus cut off the demon's head, which however had become immortal as the nectar had passed through it.

On a later occasion Śiva wished to see that enchanting form of Mohinī which had tricked the demons. He was warned that the delusory form was irresistible. Śiva, proud of his power of austerity, insisted on seeing Mohinī. But lust is the last weakness to leave one's bosom, and when Viṣṇu took on Mohinī's form Śiva was overcome by her charms and his asceticism gave way. Out of the sexual union of Śiva and Mohinī was born the divine child, Śāstha.

This story also has a mystic significance. It explains how man purifies his inner personality and reaches the state of immortality. *Mṛtam* means death and *amṛtam* means deathlessness. Deathless again means changeless. That is the state which man reaches on realisation of his Godhood.

The milky ocean represents the pure *sāttvika* mind. The gods represent the higher nature of man, the demons his lower nature. There is a constant conflict between the demands of the lower nature and the aspiration of the higher. When this conflict is resolved man seeks his supreme Self within. The serpent represents his ego and the mountain his vast experiences, *karma* in the world. He makes use of these two—his ego and his experiences—to draw the nectar of *Ātman* out of his *sāttvika* mind. The mind is first to be purified of its desires. The pure mind is then directed through the processes of assertion and negation which is the churning. The seeker asserts the supreme Self. He negates his body, mind and intellect. He directs his mind to repeat "I am *Ātman,* not the body," "I am *Ātman,* not the mind", "I am *Ātman,* not the intellect". When the mind keeps repeating the thought of *Ātman* it gets attached to it. Attachment arises out of repetition of thoughts. That is the principle of attachment. Hitherto, man has been constantly repeating that he is the body, mind and intellect. Consequently, he becomes a physical, mental and intellectual personality. He loses sight of the *Ātman.* Now when he asserts the *Atman* he becomes the *Ātman.* This is the process of evolution.

Spiritual evolution is first marked by the purging of *vāsanās,* desires symbolised by the emission of poison from the ocean. These *vāsanās* are detrimental to the well-being of mankind. They pollute the head (discrimination) and the heart (feelings). Hence, Umā arrested the poison in the throat of Śiva. She stopped it in between the head and the heart not allowing the poison to contaminate the feelings of the heart or the discrimination of the intellect.

As man evolves further in his spiritual path he acquires great powers in the world. These are represented by the attractive objects that arose out of the churning.

Thus, if the seeker continues in his spiritual pursuit he reaches the final state of Self-realisation, the bliss of Godhood, the *amṛta.*

The negative tendencies in man trade even on the spiritual treasures gained by him. Man makes use of his newly-acquired spiritual powers for low, self-aggrandising purposes. Such men fall an easy prey to the enchanting objects of the world. They are blind to their spiritual beauty. Enchanted by the senses they lose whatever wealth they have gained as the demons enchanted by Mohinī lost their nectar.

Śāstha is also known as Harihara putra, meaning the son of Hari (Viṣṇu) and Hara (Śiva). Being the son of Śiva and Viṣṇu, Śāstha has the powers of both his parents. He destroys all negative tendencies through the power of destruction gained through his father. He maintains the thought of the supreme through the power of maintenance of his mother. The devotees of Śāstha invoke these two qualities. Thus invoking the grace of Śāstha, the seeker purifies his mind and directs it to a single-pointed meditation and realisation of the Supreme.

Another name of Śāstha is Ayyappan. The Ayyappan temple in the Śabarī Hill, Kerala, is one of the most popular pilgrim centres in south India. Devotees from all over the country belonging to all creeds and classes visit this sacred shrine. Unlike other temples, the pilgrims visiting this temple have very strict and rigorous preparations to go through before reaching the divine altar. The usual custom is to observe strict austerities and self-control for forty-one days preceding the visit to the temple. By such *tapas* austerity the mind is made to withdraw its attachments to the world and slowly direct it to the thought of the Reality—*Ayyappa Svāmī Śaraṇam.* During this period of austerity, the devotee is allowed to wear only black or saffron clothes and a *mālā* rosary and strictly observe the daily rituals. The black or saffron clothes are meant to convey the pilgrim's mental resignation from the world. Black indicates darkness. The world is dark to him. The saffron colour represents fire. This indicates that his body is burnt or dead to this world. Thus with his symbolic attire the pilgrim withdraws from his mental preoccupation with the world. With such a prepared mind he cries '*Svāmī Śaraṇam*—the Lord, my refuge' all along the way to the shrine.

The way to the temple is through jungles and the pilgrimage is undertaken by foot. The idea is to further develop the concentration of the mind which has already been prepared by strict austerities. All along the ascent to the shrine, the devotee tries to maintain the one thought of the Lord in his multiple experiences. When such single-pointed concentration and meditation is maintained, the Truth reveals Itself to the seeker, which is symbolised by the *darśana* vision of the Lord in the temple.

# Brahmā

LORD BRAHMĀ is the first member of the Hindu Trinity. Viṣṇu being the second and Śiva, the third. Brahmā is the god of creation and is traditionally accepted as the Creator of the entire universe.

An individual's subtle body is constituted of his mind and intellect, that is, his entire thoughts. Man's subtle body is responsible for the creation of his gross body and also the world that he experiences. The thoughts of an individual determine the type of physical body he possesses. The same thoughts are also responsible for the type of world that the individual experiences around him. As the thoughts, so the world. If a man possesses good thoughts he sees a good world. If his thoughts are bad he sees a bad world. Yudhiṣṭhira, a virtuous man, saw virtue everywhere. While Duryodhana, a vicious man, saw vice everywhere. When thoughts are absent there is no world at all. In deep-sleep there are no thoughts, no world. This phenomenon is true not only of the microcosm but of the macrocosm as well. The cosmic subtle body is the aggregate of all subtle bodies of all living beings. The cosmic subtle body, called Hiraṇyagarbha, is said to be the creator of the entire universe. This creator is Brahmā.

The manifested world of plurality has emerged from the unmanifest Reality. To indicate this, Brahmā the creator is described as being born from the navel of Viṣṇu as he is lying on the great serpent Ananta in the milky ocean.

One of the earliest iconographic description of Brahmā is that of the four-faced god seated on a lotus. The Lord has in his four hands a *kamanḍalu* water-pot, *Vedas* sacred manuscript, *śruva* sacrificial implement and *mālā* rosary. He wears the hide of a black antelope and his vehicle is a *haṁsa* swan.

The description of Brahmā like those of other deities of Hinduism bears a mystic symbolism. The lotus represents the Reality. Brahmā sitting on the lotus indicates that he is ever-rooted in the infinite Reality. Reality is the foundation on which his personality rests. The four faces of Brahmā represent the four *Vedas.* They also represent the four ways in which thoughts function in the *antaḥkaraṇa* inner personality. The four ways in which thoughts function are: *manas* mind, *buddhi* intellect, *ahaṅkāra* ego and *cit* conditioned-consciousness. These are the manifestations of the unmanifest Consciousness.

The animal hide worn by Brahmā stands for austerity. A seeker who desires to realise his Godhead must first go through spiritual disciplines. Observing such austerities, the seeker must carefully study and reflect upon the scriptural truths which are suggested by the *Vedas* manuscript held in one hand. Having acquired the knowledge of scriptures he must work in the world without ego and egocentric desires, that is engage in dedicated and sacrificial service for the welfare of the world. This idea is suggested by the sacrificial implement held in the second hand. When a man works in

the world selflessly he drops his desires. He is no longer extroverted, materialistic, sensual. His mind is withdrawn from its preoccupations with the world of objects and beings. Such a mind is said to be in *uparati*. A man who has reached the state of *uparati* is in a spirit of renunciation. That is indicated by Brahmā holding the *kamaṇḍalu* in his hand. The *kamaṇḍalu* is a water-pot used by a *sannyāsī*—a man of renunciation. It is a symbol of *sannyāsa* or renunciation. The mind of such a man which is withdrawn from the heat of passion of the world is available for deeper concentration and meditation. The *mālā* rosary in the fourth hand is meant to be used for chanting and meditation. Meditation is the final gateway to Realisation. Through deep and consistent meditation the mind gets annihilated and the seeker attains Godhood. A God-man maintains his identity with his supreme Self while he is engaged in the world of perceptions, emotions and thoughts. He retains the concept of unity in diversity. He separates the pure unconditioned-consciousness underlying this conditioned world of names and forms. Brahmā's association with a swan is most appropriate in this context. A swan is described in Hindu mysticism as possessing the unique faculty of separating pure milk from a mixture of milk and water. It is reputed to have the ability to draw the milk alone and leave the water behind. So does a Man-of-Realisation move about in the world recognising the one Divinity in the pluralistic phenomena of the world.

Brahmā is said to be the Lord of creation. The creator must necessarily possess the knowledge to create. Without knowledge no creation is possible. Hence Brahmā is said to be wedded to the goddess of knowledge, Sarasvatī. Life in this world is a manifestation of the three principles of creation, sustenance and destruction. In fact these three are interconnected. The apparent destruction is only an essential forerunner to creation. Destruction and creation go hand in hand. They are like two sides of a coin. For example, the destruction of morning is creation of noon and the destruction of noon is creation of night. This chain of continuous destruction and construction maintains the day. Similarly, the destruction of childhood is the creation of youth and the destruction of youth the creation of old age. In this process of birth and death the individual is maintained. Hence, the three gods of the Trinity viz. Brahmā, Viṣṇu and Śiva representing creation, maintenance and destruction, are essentially one and the same.

The above idea is well portrayed in Lord Dattātreya, in whose form the three gods are combined. Dattātreya has the three faces of Brahmā, Viṣṇu and Śiva to indicate that the three principles for which they stand are inseparable. Lord Dattātreya is shown with four dogs following him. The four dogs represent the four Vedas. A dog is one of the most faithful animals in the world and it follows its master in all environments and circumstances. So, too, the Vedas are said to follow a Man-of-Realisation in the sense that all his actions, thoughts and desires are in perfect accord with the principles enunciated in the Vedic texts.

All creations arise out of *vikṣepa* thought-disturbances. This *vikṣepaśakti* is Lord Brahmā—the total mind-intellect equipment. Man, being essentially constituted of his mind and intellect, has already invoked this *vikṣepaśakti* and realised Brahmā. Hence the worship and invocation of Brahmā is practised by few.

Yet there are a few shrines dedicated to Brahmā. He is worshipped and invoked particularly by scientists and kings for generating more creative ideas to serve the world of men and matter. The rulers invoke the Lord in order to surrender their ego and produce plans and schemes to serve the nation. Similarly, the research scholars invoke creative inspiration and flashes of new thoughts revealing the secrets of nature.

Lord Brahmā is not popularly worshipped in India. This is so because the idea of creation is repugnant to seekers of Truth, since the creation of thoughts has veiled the infinite Reality. The attempt of all spiritual seekers is to destroy the existing thoughts and maintain the state of single-pointed thought until the Reality is revealed. Hence, Śiva (god of destruction) and Viṣṇu (god of maintenance) are worshipped more than Brahmā. In fact, there are very few temples of Brahmā—one in Rajasthan and another in Orissa—compared to innumerable shrines of Śiva and Viṣṇu existing all over India.

# Consorts of the Three Gods

*SARASVATĪ:* Goddess of Knowledge

The Vedic tradition of India from time immemorial has given women the highest place of respect and recognition. The Hindu scriptures are referred to as Mother Śruti and the Bhagavad Gītā as Mother Gītā. Knowledge itself has been personified as a feminine deity—the Goddess Sarasvatī. Sarasvatī literally means "one who gives the *sāra* essence of *sva* own Self".

The goddess Sarasvatī is represented as sitting on a lotus. She holds the sacred scripture in one hand and a lotus in the other. With the third and fourth hands she plays the *vīṇā,* Indian lute.

The seat of the lotus indicates that the goddess is firmly established in the experience of the supreme Reality. She is rooted in Truth which the lotus represents. By holding the lotus in her hand Sarasvatī indicates to man the supreme Goal that he should reach in his lifetime, the goal of Self-realisation. The path of that goal is shown by her other hands. There are two distinct paths taking man to the highest experience, Godhood—the path of knowledge and the path of devotion.

The path of knowledge is shown by the goddess holding the sacred book. It is called *jñāna mārga* in Sanskrit. It expounds Vedānta, the philosophy of the Vedas. It is a systematic and scientific presentation of the realities of life. It explains the various layers of matter that man possesses and the core of Reality that lies beneath them. By careful study and reflection the seeker unravels the mystery of his inner life until he reaches the core of his supreme Self. This path is meant for the intellectuals.

The path of devotion is called *bhakti mārga.* This path also leads to the goal of Self-realisation. This is meant for those who are predominantly devotional, who use their heart to sing praises of their Lord. Through music, *kīrtans* or *bhajans* they maintain a single-pointed devotion to the Lord and thereby attain Godhood. This is indicated by Sarasvatī playing the *vīṇā.*

The four hands of the goddess represent the four aspects of the inner personality of man namely *manas* mind, *buddhi* intellect, *ahankāra* ego and *citta* conditioned-consciousness.

Sarasvatī is the consort of Brahmā. Brahmā is the creator. Creation is not possible unless the creator has the knowledge of what and how to create. Knowledge therefore is an essential prerequisite for creation. This idea is symbolised by wedding Brahmā and Sarasvatī.

During the nine-day festival of *devīpūjā* goddess-worships, Goddess Kālī (Durgā) is worshipped on the first three days, Goddess Lakṣmī on the next three days and Sarasvatī on the last three days. Kālī represents the power of destruction. By invoking Kālī the devotee is said to draw her mighty power to destroy all his negative tendencies.

Thereafter, the worship of Lakṣmī, the goddess of wealth, is meant to cultivate and preserve a person's noble qualities like self-control, tolerance, love etc. These are his inner wealth. Having cleansed the inner personality of the negativities and substituting them with positive qualities the devotee is qualified to receive the knowledge of the Self. The study of the scriptures is futile if one approaches it with an unclean mind. An unclean mind is ever agitated. Such a mind is not fit for study and reflection upon the highest truths of life. A pure mind and an enquiring intellect directed to research of the Self together bring about spiritual awakening. This is symbolised by the devotee worshipping Goddess Sarasvatī on the last three days. On the tenth day an effigy is burnt or thrown into the sea to indicate the destruction of the ego, the annihilation of the lower nature of man. That day is the day of enlightenment, *Vidyārambha.*

*LAKṢMĪ:* Goddess of Wealth

Lakṣmī is the consort of Lord Viṣṇu. Viṣṇu represents the power of maintenance. In order to manifest this power Viṣṇu must necessarily possess wealth. Even in the world a person who is in charge of maintenance needs wealth. A pauper cannot maintain anything. Viṣṇu is the maintainer of the entire universe, hence is married to the goddess of wealth.

Lakṣmī is said to be *svarṇa hasta,* meaning golden-handed. As the name suggests the goddess pours out riches to the community. Where there is Lakṣmī there is prosperity. Wealth here also includes moral and ethical values, the nobler aspects of life, the power of the mind and intellect. This kind of wealth has to be acquired by a seeker before his

initiation into spiritual knowledge. That explains why Lakṣmī is worshipped before Sarasvatī during the *devīpūjā*.

Wealth however does not come to a person by merely begging at the feet of Lakṣmī. Worship of Lakṣmī these days has become mere solicitation of material wealth. Man does not realise that when he runs after wealth it moves away from him. The way to command wealth is to leave it alone and to seek the higher values of life. This idea is well-brought out in the allegory of the churning of the milky ocean. The ocean of milk represents a *sāttvika* pure mind. When man contemplates with a pure mind on the higher ideals of life he evolves spiritually. By gradual evolution he reaches the goal of Perfection. A man of Perfection gains everything in the world. He commands peace, power and prosperity. Wealth is at his feet. This is the way to gain wealth, to win over Lakṣmī. Lakṣmī emerging by the churning of the milky ocean symbolises this truth.

Lakṣmī is described as being seated on a lotus. She holds a lotus in her hand. This is a common symbol amongst most of the Hindu gods and goddesses. It only means they are well-rooted in the supreme Reality. By holding a lotus in their hands they only point out to mankind that the goal of their existence is Realisation of the inner wealth.

### *GODDESS PĀRVATĪ*

Pārvatī is the consort of Lord Śiva. Śiva represents the power of the destruction. Pārvatī is also known as Umā. Umā represents *prakṛti* matter. Matter is destructible. The power of destruction can manifest itself only where there is destructible matter. Destruction ceases to have any meaning

without destructible objects. Śiva being the Lord of destruction is necessarily wedded to Umā to manifest the power of destruction.

Pārvatī is also referred to as *annapūrnī* which means 'bestower of food'. *Anna* means 'food', which is to be taken in a wider connotation. To mean food for all sense organs i.e. all sense-objects.

*GODDESS DURGĀ*

The other forms of Pārvatī are Durgā and Kālī which are awesome and terrifying. In these forms the goddess rides a lion, wields a number of weapons and wears a garland of skulls, holds a severed head in one hand and a lotus in another etc. All these represent destruction of evil and protection of good (lotus). This goddess is therefore invoked by the seeker to destroy all his *vāsanās* desires and unveil his supreme Self.

Man at present is riddled with innumerable desires, agitations and sufferings. He is tormented by his own negative thoughts and feelings such as selfishness, jealousy, hatred, greed etc. These are the greatest enemies in man's bosom which loot his inner peace and bliss. They have to be totally annihilated for man to reach the abode of everlasting happiness. Even as he destroys a few of his sins more spring up in the same form. They grow and spread like bacteria and destroy his peace and tranquillity. There is no room for persuasion or softness in dealing with these arch enemies of man. They have to be ruthlessly struck and destroyed. By worshipping Durgā this idea of ruthless destruction is invoked to annihilate all the desires and unfold Divinity.

# Kṛṣṇa

KṚṢṆA was a dynamic incarnation of Lord Viṣṇu. He was an *Avatāra*. An *Avatāra* is one who is attuned to the supreme Consciousness from birth. Kṛṣṇa's incarnation brought about a profound and powerful influence upon Indian thought and life. There is no aspect of Indian life, culture and civilisation which does not receive his revitalising touch. India's philosophy and religion, mysticism and poetry, painting and sculpture, music and dance articulated Kṛṣṇa's theme and thought. Every aspect of Kṛṣṇa's life and deeds has a mystic symbolism indicating a sublime truth. Some of them are explained below. They should set a direction to the reader for deeper study and discovery of the allegorical significance of the entire story of Kṛṣṇa.

Kṛṣṇa in Sanskrit means dark. Kṛṣṇa represents the inner Self, *Ātman*. The *Ātman* is dark in the sense that it is unknown to man as long as he is involved in his terrestrial experiences. Man's knowledge is limited to the realms of perceptions, emotions and thoughts. He gains these experiences through his three equipments of body, mind and intellect. He knows not the *Ātman* within. The body, mind and intellect by themselves are inert and insentient. They constitute the material aspect of man. The *Ātman* is his spiritual being. The *Ātman* is the living principle in man which transforms his inert matter into a living being.

Kṛṣṇa is blue in colour and wears yellow clothes. Blue colour has always been associated with infinity. The sky appears blue. So does the ocean. Yellow colour represents earth. When sand is introduced in a colourless flame, the flame turns yellow. The blue form of Kṛṣṇa clothed in yellow therefore suggests the infinite Reality reduced to a finite human being. The incarnation of Kṛṣṇa represents the descent of God on earth. This idea of the limitless, formless Reality being constricted and restricted to a limited, human form is again suggested by Kṛṣṇa's birth in a prison. The divine child was however not confined to the prison. No sooner was Kṛṣṇa born than the prison doors miraculously flung open. The guards could not hold the child back. The child's father, Vasudeva, carried him out of the prison in spite of the severe restrictions imposed on him. This episode is meant to convey that the infinite Being can never be really restricted or limited to the human form. A Godman is ever free and liberated. The *Ātman* in man is limitless. Only his body, mind and intellect are limited, finite. These material equipments have a beginning and an end. They cannot restrict the *Ātman.* The *Ātman* is eternal, all-pervading, infinite. Kṛṣṇa represents that *Ātman.*

Kṛṣṇa was born in Mathurā. His uncle, Kaṁsa was a tyrant. Kaṁsa imprisoned his father and usurped the throne of Mathurā. He reigned over Mathurā. His minister Chāṇūra was equally wicked and cruel. Under the rule of these two tyrants Mathurā suffered greatly from confusion and chaos. Kṛṣṇa destroyed them both and restored peace and order in that land. The word *madhuram* means sweetness. The land of Mathurā represents the personality of man. Man's essential nature is his *Ātman.* His real nature

is ever sweet, peaceful and blissful. But when the evil forces of ego and egocentric desires usurp man's personality he suffers from stress and strain, worries and anxieties. He is agitated and sorrowful. He loses his blissful nature. To regain the lost bliss man has to destroy his ego and egocentric desires and establish his identity with his supreme Self.

There is a Purāṇic story which speaks of Kṛṣṇa killing a mighty serpent with many heads. It lived in a lake poisoning its water. The entire village suffered because of this dragon. Kṛṣṇa jumped into the lake and began to crush down its heads. But as he crushed them other heads sprung up in their place. Kṛṣṇa ultimately crushed all the heads and vanquished the serpent. He danced on its crested head playing the flute. The wives of the dragon paid homage to the Lord.

This story again has an allegorical significance. The lake represents the mind. The dragon and its many heads the ego and egocentric desires. The ego and egocentric desires poison the mind and make its world miserable. When man turns his attention inward, when he contemplates and meditates upon his *Ātman,* upon Kṛṣṇa he overcomes his ego and egocentric desires. Thereafter he revels in the bliss of Realisation. The sense-objects of the world become subservient to such a man. This is symbolised by the wives of the serpent paying homage to Kṛṣṇa.

Kṛṣṇa is often represented as playing a flute. The enchanting music emanating from the flute of the lord is the bliss of Godhood enjoyed by the Man-of-Realisation. The flute is hollow but it can produce enchanting music. So too when man empties himself of his *vāsanās* and desires the Divinity within him flows out with enchanting bliss. Man has to give up all his claims upon his body, mind and intellect, give up all his egocentric connections, all thoughts of 'mine' and 'thine', rise above them all and chant *Om* (Kṛṣṇa), remove all selfishness from the flute of his body and fill it with the divine breath of *Om*. Man becomes God.

The milkmaids of Brindāvan were called *gopīs*. These *gopīs* were enchanted by the divine music flowing out of Kṛṣṇa's flute. They danced in their ecstasy around Kṛṣṇa. The dance of the *gopīs* is known as *rāsa-līlā*. Kṛṣṇa again represents the *Ātman,* pure Consciousness while *gopīs* represent thoughts. *Ātman* in man is the enlivening factor by which he becomes conscious of his thoughts. Thoughts by themselves are insentient. In the presence of Consciousness thoughts gain sentiency or consciousness. Thoughts dance around the *Ātman* as it were. But the *Ātman* is ever-immaculate. It is unaffected by the thoughts around it. So is Kṛṣṇa pure, immaculate. He remains detached and unaffected by the dancing *gopīs*. Losing this allegorical significance of the *rāsa-līlā* much criticism has been levelled against Kṛṣṇa's association with the *gopīs*. The *gopīs* were in fact deeply devoted to Lord Kṛṣṇa. They remembered Kṛṣṇa throughout the day in all their activities. Their limbs were ceaselessly engaged in their obligatory duties while their minds were constantly attuned to the Lord. To dedicate oneself to a higher being and work in the world without ego and egocentric desires is *karma yoga*. When man works in a spirit of *karma yoga* he gets rid of his *vāsanās,* desires. This idea is suggested by Kṛṣṇa stealing the butter which the *gopīs* had churned and collected in their pots. The desire for realisation of the Self alone remains. This last trace of desire gets eliminated by itself through single-pointed meditation upon the Lord. In Verse 66 of Chapter XVIII of the Bhagavad Gītā the Lord gives man this assurance:

> "Abandoning all *dharmas,* take refuge in Me alone, I will liberate thee from all sins, grieve not."

There is yet another beautiful incident in Kṛṣṇa's life indicating his absolute state of detachment. It served as an eye-opener to the two wives of Kṛṣṇa when they began to doubt his association with many *gopīs.*

One day the great sage Durvāsa camped with his many disciples on the opposite bank of river Yamunā where Kṛṣṇa lived. Kṛṣṇa's wives saw the sage and prepared a lot of sweetmeats to take to him. In the evening when both the ladies with their trays of delicacies approached the river it was flooded. They could not cross over to the other bank to make the offering to the sage. They returned and sought Kṛṣṇa's help. Kṛṣṇa asked them to go back to the river-side and pray to Mother Yamunā (the rivers in India are deified as goddesses), "If sage Durvāsa is a *nitya upavāsī* please show us the way". *Nitya* means eternal, permanent. *Upavāsī* means one who fasts. So *nitya upavāsī* is one who is always observing fast. The ladies did not understand the implication. They followed Kṛṣṇa's advice and prayed to Goddess Yamunā. The goddess granted their prayer and instantly the waters subsided. They crossed over and offered the sweets to the sage. The sage ate every bit of the food and returned the empty trays. A *nitya upavāsī!*

Kṛṣṇa's wives took the sage's blessings and reached the river bank to return home. Again, the river was flooded preventing them from crossing over. This time they sought the help of Durvāsa. The sage advised them to go back to the river bank and pray to goddess Yamunā, "If Kṛṣṇa is a *nitya brahmacārī* please show us the way". *Nitya brahmacārī* means permanent celibate. The ladies followed the advice and prayed to the Yamunā. To their amazement the waters subsided forthwith enabling them to cross over to the other bank.

The significance of this episode is obvious. Durvāsa was totally free from mental attachment to any type of food. He had absolutely no desire or craving for them. Eating to him was a ritual, an obligatory function. Such a person though eating eats not. A man of perfect detachment "even though acting acts not" (Bhagavad Gītā Chapter IV, Verse 20). Durvāsa belonged to that rare category. He was ever mentally detached from food. Hence he was called a *nitya upavāsī* even as he was eating like any other man.

The same principle applies to Kṛṣṇa. It is not man's physical expression but his mental impression that determines his attachment or detachment to the world. Kṛṣṇa's association with the *gopīs* did not in any way affect his total detachment, his mental resignation from them. He was ever maintaining an inward dispassion and disinterest even as he was closely associating with the *gopīs.* His mind was ever in a state of *brahmacarya* celibacy. Hence he was called a *nitya brahmacārī*.

In his childhood, Kṛṣṇa is said to have eaten mud on an occasion. His mother Yaśodā chided him. Kṛṣṇa denied having eaten mud. Yaśodā would not take his word. She asked him to open his mouth. The child did so. Yaśodā was wonderstruck to see the entire universe within the child's mouth. This episode has a deep philosophical implication. Kṛṣṇa is the Infinite, Omnipresent, Omnipotent Reality. The Reality alone exists. Nothing else does. The universe is nothing but the same Reality, though seen differently by men with limited vision. Yaśodā was one of those who could not see the supreme Being in Kṛṣṇa. She only saw her child in him. But in truth Kṛṣṇa is that all-pervading Reality which includes the earth as well. The earth is a part of the Reality which Kṛṣṇa is. Kṛṣṇa therefore gave the right answer to his mother when he denied eating earth. How can Kṛṣṇa (Reality) eat mud (Reality)? Kṛṣṇa was therefore speaking the Truth. When Yaśodā insisted on knowing the truth Kṛṣṇa had to reveal it by opening his mouth and showing the universe in Him.

Man's essential nature is the supreme Reality. The world is also nothing but Reality. Yet man finds the necessity to run after the world of objects for his pleasures. Is this not an absurd situation — Reality in the form of man craving to enjoy Reality in the form of the world? This absurdity of man's pursuit is subtly implied when Kṛṣṇa as a baby is shown sucking his own big toe.

Lord Kṛṣṇa is also described as holding a staff in one hand and showing a symbol of wisdom, *jñāna mudrā* with the other. A staff is used by a cowherd boy to drive the cattle to the pasture lands for grazing. The *jñāna mudrā* is a symbol made by holding the little, ring and middle fingers erect and bringing the index finger to touch the middle portion of the thumb. This again has a philosophical meaning. Kṛṣṇa represents the *Ātman* in man. *Ātman* is the Life-Principle which enlivens his body, mind and intellect. Without the life spark man cannot act at all. All actions are possible because of the life spark. Actions broadly classified fall under two distinct heads — actions that are degrading and devolutionary and those that are elevating and evolutionary. Man can make use of the *Ātman* to evolve or to devolve. *Ātman* is neutral. It helps man to pursue whatever direction he wants. The first type of actions is indicated by Kṛṣṇa holding the staff. The cattle represents the sense organs. The sense organs constantly feed upon the sense-objects of the world. Eyes go to colour and form, ears go to sound, the tongue to taste etc. The sense-objects are the pastures for the sense organs. Man spends all his life driving his sense organs to their respective fields of enjoyment for sensual pleasures. He uses his Life-Principle merely to indulge in sense gratification. That seems to be his main occupation in life.

The other type of actions, indicated by the *jñāna mudrā,* leads man to Self-realisation. The index finger represents the ego. It is the pointing finger which creates duality, plurality. Man develops his ego by his association and identification with his body, mind and intellect, with his gross, subtle and causal bodies, with his *sāttvika, rājasika* and *tāmasika guṇas.* This idea is indicated by the index finger remaining in contact with the other three fingers.

The thumb represents the *Ātman* by virtue of the vital role it plays in all actions. The index finger bending towards the thumb to form a circle shows the ego's detachment from the three bodies or *guṇas* and total surrender to the *Ātman.* When man does that he reaches his Infinite state, the state of Self-realisation. This state of Infinitude is indicated by making a circle. The circle has no beginning or end. That which has no beginning or end is said to be infinite. Kṛṣṇa gives this choice of action to man, that is to spend his lifetime in merely gratifying his senses or to transcend the limitations of his body, mind and intellect and reach the state of Realisation. Kṛṣṇa is a mere witness, a *sākṣī.* He does not interfere with your choice. He merely presents the truth for you to decide your course of life. In the *Bhagavad Gītā,* Arjuna surrenders to Kṛṣṇa completely and seeks his advice. Kṛṣṇa gives him the entire philosophy of life in the eighteen chapters of the Gītā. Towards the end of the last chapter he declares to Arjuna, "I have declared the highest wisdom to you, reflect upon it and act as you choose to".

# Rāma

LORD RĀMA stands out as the most glorious of all characters found in scriptural literature. In the Rāmāyaṇa Sage Vālmīki has symbolised Rāma as an ideal of perfection. No other character has been described with such idealistic perfection displayed in **all** aspects of life in a single individual.

The human personality consists of different facets functioning in diverse aspects of life. In most human beings only one or two of these facets are well-developed. The rest lack perfection. In the life of Rāma each facet of human personality is seen projected to absolute perfection. Thus, the various roles that Rāma played in his lifetime were of idealistic perfection. He was a perfect son, an ideal king, a true husband, a real friend, a devoted brother, a noble enemy etc. While painting the picture of each facet of his personality, Vālmīki would not compromise with its highest standard of perfection. Consequently when the sage high-lighted one facet of Rāma's personality to absolute Perfection he could not do justice to other aspects. That explains why some critics read certain apparent inconsistencies in the divine character of Rāma.

One such instance is the criticism levelled against Rāma for leaving his aged father, King Daśaratha, and going away to the forest. Daśaratha was protesting against

Rāma's departure from the palace. Rāma himself knew that his father would not survive the sorrow of his exile, yet Rāma left. This criticism has no bearing when one understands the role that Rāma was playing at that time. Sage Vālmīki was depicting Rāma in that episode as an ideal son to a father. An exaggerated situation was created purposely to highlight the greatness of the **son** in Rāma. Consider the facts of the situation. It was the eve of Rāma's coronation. All the subjects of Ayodhyā were eagerly waiting for the coronation of the young king. And Rāma himself was aware of his duty to them. His stepmother Kaikeyī's demand to have his younger brother Bharata crowned and Rāma sent away to the forest was preposterous, to say the least, in the light of the irresistible love that his parents bore for him and he for them. In spite of all these extreme challenges Rāma stood out as a real son. Discharging a son's duty to fulfil the father's promise in spite of the insurmountable obstacles. Rāma would not compromise with the fulfilment of his duty as a true son. All other considerations were kept aside while this aspect of his character was highlighted. That is the way one has to study and appreciate the beauty of Rāma's character.

Another common criticism of Rāma's character is his action in sending away his queen Sītā to the forest in response to an irresponsible prattle of a washerman questioning the purity of the queen. Here again one aspect of Rāma's personality is highlighted almost to a point of fault and that is his ideal kingship. An ideal king in those days was one who was accepted by all his subjects unlike the present system of majority, or at times minority rule. So when King Rāma heard a single dissenting voice against

him, he made the greatest sacrifice in sending his queen away. This action of Rāma, though apparently absurd, portrays the sanctity that he attached to accepted standards of ideal kingship in his days.

In striking contrast to this gesture you find the deep concern of a husband in Rāma when Sītā was carried away by Rāvaṇa. In that situation Rāma displayed the ideal husband that he was. He put forth superhuman efforts until he regained Sītā.

Another serious criticism of Rāma's character is his apparent cowardice when he hid behind a tree to shoot his arrow at Vāli. Vāli and Sugrīva were kings of the monkeys. Vāli was the vicious king who threw his brother Sugrīva out and usurped the throne. On Sugrīva's representation to Rāma, Rāma devised a plan to help him out of his troubles. He bade Sugrīva challenge his brother and fight him. As the fight was in progress Rāma shot down Vāli from his hiding place behind a tree. Here again is the friend in Rāma blown up to a point of fault. Rāma would go to any extent to help a friend. Besides this character being demonstrated there is a deeper mystical significance in this episode which Vālmīki is trying to convey to mankind.

Vāli, the vicious and immoral brother, represents lust, the lower nature of man. Sugrīva, the virtuous and moral brother, represents man's higher nature. Vāli is said to have gone through extensive austerity, *tapas* and earned a boon. By this boon he acquired half the strength of the adversary whom he met in battle. Consequently, he was able to overpower anyone because half the strength gained thereby plus his own was always more than that of the opponent. All this was meant to convey that the sense-objects of the world are extremely powerful. The power of lust has toppled great minds. The moment man comes in contact with the sense-objects the latter draws away half his strength and overpowers him. Man becomes a slave to his own senses. In this episode Vālmīki suggests to mankind the means of overcoming the power of lust. As long as man is in the midst of sense-objects it is extremely difficult to exercise his control and overcome temptations. The way to deal with them successfully is to stay away from them initially until he gains sufficient control over them. This is a practical approach to self-control. It is not to be construed as escapism. When a man is already under the influence of the senses he cannot afford to mix freely with the sense- objects in question. The initial abstinence is therefore recommended as a practical approach to gain the control over them. Once man gains self-control he can then afford to mix freely with the sense-objects. This idea is communicated by Rāma avoiding Vāli and shooting him from a distance.

Lord Rāma carried his bow and arrows all the time. This symbolises his alertness and readiness to fight against iniquity and thus establish justice and peace. Iniquity will always be there in this world. By his example Rāma gives mankind strength and conviction to fight it. Man ought not to be weak and accept unrighteousness passively. He has to rise actively against anything that is inconsistent or contrary to righteousness or morality. That is called aggressive goodness. Rāma, Kṛṣṇa and all other gods wielded weapons which symbolised this quality that man needs to develop. They stand for righteousness and oppose and destroy all that is unrighteous. Thus, throughout the Rāmāyaṇa there are several such actions and anecdotes expressing the divine brilliance of the ideal personality of Lord Rāma.

# PART II
## Epics, Rituals and Festivals

# The Mahābhārata

Sage Vyāsa, the celebrated compiler of the Vedas, also contributed the epic poem Mahābhārata to the world. The Mahābhārata is a divine work recounting great deeds of godlike heroes of the golden age of India. Besides the main story there are several short yet immortal anecdotes and endless surmises, theology, philosophy, natural sciences, law, worldly and spiritual knowledge of life. The kernel of the great epic is the Bhagavad Gītā which establishes the existence of the highest Truth and prescribes different techniques to recognise It.

The important characters of this seemingly terrestrial drama and the events depicted therein have a deeper significance. The epic has a message for mankind which is of far greater importance than its mere story on the mundane plane. It portrays to man his own lower self, *jīva* with all its terrestrial problems, as well as his higher Self, *Ātman* with Its transcendental glory. It explains how to merge the little self with the greater Self and bring about the all-embracing synthesis of man and God. The great works of Indian arts and literature — be they the Mahābhārata or the Rāmāyaṇa or the images of gods and goddesses — are all infused with the idea of penetrating the terrestrial realm and discovering the transcendental Truth beyond it.

The central narrative describes the rivalry between two branches of a royal family, known as the Pāṇḍavas and Kauravas. The jealous and vicious Kauravas led the Pāṇḍavas finally to a fratricidal war which ends in an all but complete extinction of that large family along with their allies and supporters.

Kṛṣṇa represents the *Ātman.* The *Ātman* is the inner Self, the Life-Spark in man. *Ātman* is the source of all actions be they noble or ignoble. Both good and bad actions are not possible without the presence of *Ātman* within. *Ātman* however is not in any way responsible for the quality of the actions emanating from it. It is as it were a silent witness of all types of activities projected by the body, mind and intellect. This idea is brought out in the *Udyogaparva* where Kṛṣṇa is asleep while Duryodhana and Arjuna sit on either side waiting to advance their claims for help in the impending war, each hoping to secure Kṛṣṇa's help exclusively for himself. Kṛṣṇa wakes up and satisfies both the parties by giving his armies to Duryodhana and his personal service, unarmed, to Arjuna. From the metaphysical plane, this episode conveys that the *daivika* noble and the *āsurī* ignoble forces symbolised by Arjuna and Duryodhana both derive their power from the primeval Source which by Itself has no activity (Kṛṣṇa sleeping) to its credit or discredit. In other words the *Ātman* or Consciousness is the substratum from which all activities, good or evil, emanate but Itself remains pure or uncontaminated by any such activities.

The Pāṇḍava hero, Arjuna and the Yādava chieftain, Kṛṣṇa are also represented as incarnations of the two sages

Nara and Nārāyaṇa. *Nara* stands for man and *Nārāyaṇa* for the supreme Being. Thus the pair represents man and God, *jīvātma* and *Paramātma*. Arjuna fighting the Kaurava army is indicative of the efforts put in by the *jīvātma*, the lower self, the empirical ego. To conquer its desires and passions, hatred and greed, envy and malice and a host of other negative tendencies. This conquest is made possible by the *jīva*'s association with the divine Self.

The homeland of this royal family was sacred and blissful — a *Dharmakṣetra*, as long as the Pāṇḍavas were reigning over it. No sooner did the blind king Dhṛtarāṣṭra and his hundred wicked sons take over the kingdom than there was a complete change in policy from the spiritual to the secular and consequent fall in integrity of character culminating in the disastrous war of Kurukṣetra. The king was blind by birth but the queen denied herself the use of her eyes by voluntarily tying a piece of cloth around her eyes as a mark of subservience to her blind husband. *Dharmakṣetra* represents the divine and blissful nature of man because of the presence of the supreme Self within. The mind of man is however blind to his infinite Stature. It is ignorant of the supreme Self. Its ignorance changes man's blissful state to a stormy field of strifes and struggles, trials and tribulations, worries and anxieties. The intellect also, blindly following the mind, denies to itself the capacity to rise to spiritual heights and apprehend the pure Self.

The mind and intellect are constituted of thoughts. The hundred wicked sons of Dhṛtarāṣṭra, the Kauravas, represent vicious thoughts and emotions: lust, greed, hatred, anger, envy, pride, vanity etc. The five Pāṇḍavas stand for virtuous thoughts and emotions: love, kindness, sympathy etc. The negative propensities in man generally outnumber his positive propensities. The civil war of Kurukṣetra hints at the psychological conflict between these two opposing forces in the human personality. In short, it points to the perpetual war between the higher and lower nature of man.

It is interesting to know that the Pāṇḍava army, though smaller in number, ultimately established its victory over the larger army of the Kauravas. The Pāṇḍavas however owed their victory to Lord Kṛṣṇa. On the battlefield when Arjuna collapsed in a hysterical coma, laid down his bow and arrows and surrendered to Lord Kṛṣṇa for guidance, the Lord administered the great message of the Bhagavad Gītā in the chariot positioned between the two armies. The Gītā revived and recharged the Pāṇḍava prince with a higher vision. Consequently Arjuna fought the battle and emerged victorious. The victory symbolises the revival of the spiritual values of Indian culture.

The goal of human evolution is realisation of the *Ātman*, the inner Self. The *Ātman* lies beyond the realms of the good and bad. Good and bad are relative terms, the *Ātman* is absolute. Goodness is gained as a result of virtuous actions which are propelled by pure and noble emotions. Similarly, badness is the result of vicious actions propelled by impure and ignoble emotions. In both cases actions emanate from emotions rather than higher intellectual discrimination. Such actions always create desires or *vāsanās* which veil the *Ātman*. For unveiling the *Ātman*, man has to purify his mind and apply his intellect detachedly towards the higher following the guidelines of the Gītā. This idea is well brought out by Arjuna, the purified one, standing in between the armies of the good and the bad and receiving the message of the Gītā from Lord Kṛṣṇa.

The chariot in which Arjuna rides in the battle is also significant. The metaphor of the chariot is taken from the Kaṭhopaniṣad. Kṛṣṇa is the charioteer. The chariot and horses represent the human body and its five sense organs. The reins represent the mind and charioteer represents the intellect. The rider is the *jīva* individual, or the ego in man. When the charioteer is asleep the reins become loose and the horses go out of control resulting in the destruction of both the chariot and rider. So too, when man's intellect is not alert the mind loses control over the senses which leads the individual to disaster. The chariot well-controlled by the charioteer therefore represents a self-controlled man who alone can understand and derive the benefit from spiritual instructions.

The Mahābhārata therefore is not a mere story of a war fought between two armies. It picturises an everlasting cosmic drama wherein men and women are actors and actresses taking sides in the conflict between right and wrong, between good and evil, justice and injustice and playing their own appointed parts. However, the sum and substance of the epic is that man's real friend and enemy are both within him, not outside. They are his higher spiritual aspirations and his lower sensual desires. The Lord advises man to fight and conquer his great enemy and thus regain his lost glory, the pure Self, Kṛṣṇa within.

# The Rāmāyaṇa

THE RĀMĀYAṆA is a great epic of the Hindus. The epical narrative with its many stories, anecdotes and incidents explains how man has fallen from his supreme state of peace and bliss to his limited existence of sorrow and misery and how he regains his original glory.

As the story goes, King Daśaratha lived in Ayodhyā with his three queens Kausalyā, Sumitrā and Kaikeyī. They lived a life of peace and contentment. Daśaratha means a man who has controlled his ten senses. The three wives represent the three mental qualities, the *sāttvika, rājasika* and *tāmasika guṇas.* To a self-controlled man the three *guṇas* are at his service. In contrast a man who has no control over his senses is victimised by his own *guṇas.* Lord Rāma was born into such a house of self-control, peace and contentment. Sītā was married to Rāma. Both Rāma and Sītā lived happily in Daśaratha's palace in Ayodhyā. With all the royal comforts and amenities of the palace at her disposal Sītā was always single-pointedly devoted to her divine husband. She was ever content and happy. As days passed by, King Daśaratha decided to retire leaving his kingdom to his eldest son Rāma to rule. The coronation day was fixed. All of Ayodhyā was revelling in ecstasy. Just on the eve of the coronation Kaikeyī, the stepmother of Rāma, demanded the two boons that Daśaratha had given her. Firstly, that Rāma be sent away to the jungle for fourteen years. Secondly, that her son, Bharata, be crowned king instead of Rāma. Consequently, Rāma left Ayodhyā followed by Sītā and Lakṣmaṇa. In the jungle Sītā remained devoted to her Lord Rāma. She continued to live with the same contentment and happiness which she enjoyed in the palace at Ayodhyā.

The significance of this portion of the story is that man is very happy and contented as long as he is attuned to the inner Self. All the sorrows of man are caused by his preoccupation with the external world. Rāma represents the *Ātman*, the supreme Self and Sītā the ego, the individual.

As long as Sītā's attention was on Rāma she was ever blissful be it in the luxuries of the palace or the exigencies of the jungle. Similarly, if man's attention and interest are upon the inner Self and not the enchantment of the world, he would remain ever peaceful and happy whether he be placed in a state of prosperity or penury.

One day Sītā saw a beautiful golden deer in the jungle. She was enchanted. She desired to possess it. She pleaded with Rāma to capture it for her. Lakṣmaṇa warned her that the beautiful deer was a *rākṣasa* demon in disguise. Sītā turned a deaf ear. She insisted on having it. Rāma yielded and went after the animal. The deer was in fact a *rākṣasa.* It led Rāma far away from their hut. Rāma shot it with his arrow. The deer fell and as it was dying it shouted the names of Lakṣmaṇa and Sītā, as if to indicate that Rāma was in trouble. Sītā heard the cry and bade Lakṣmaṇa rush to the scene to help his brother. Lakṣmaṇa again warned her that it was a trick being played on them by the *rākṣasa* but Sītā would not heed the words of Lakṣmaṇa. Lakṣmaṇa therefore had to leave her alone in the hut and go. As Lakṣmaṇa disappeared into the jungle a mendicant with a begging bowl appeared before Sītā. That mendicant was Rāvaṇa, the ten-headed *rākṣasa* in disguise. Rāvaṇa carried Sītā away to Laṅkā.

The meaning of this portion is simple. Man is contented and happy as long as his attention and concentration are upon his real Self. The moment he looks out extrovertedly at the sense-objects of the world he develops a desire. The golden deer represents the fascinating sense-objects like colour and form for the eyes, sound for the ears, taste for the tongue, smell for the nose and touch for the skin. The joys derived from the sense-objects are transient, fleeting. They swiftly pass away like the deer. And yet man falls a prey to their golden enchantment and becomes a slave to his own sense organs — the five organs of perception and the five organs of action. He becomes a captive of the ten-headed Rāvaṇa as it were.

In Laṅkā Sītā refused to enter the golden palace of Rāvaṇa. She chose to stay in the garden of the *Aśoka* trees called the *Aśokavana.* There she remained, away from Rāvaṇa. Sītā was tempted with gifts. She was harassed with threats but she would not deviate from her unswerving devotion for her Lord Rāma. As days passed by, her devotion and dedication to Rāma were rewarded by the appearance of Hanumān, the messenger of Rāma. Hanumān gave Sītā a ring as the token from Rāma. Sītā was overjoyed and thereafter gained supreme confidence in her reunion with Rāma. With the renewed faith and confidence she continued to contemplate upon her Lord until Rāma came and liberated her.

This part of the Rāmāyaṇa symbolises the ways and means of liberation for mankind from his abject slavery to his sense organs, to his sovereign state of Godhood. Sītā's refusal to enter Rāvaṇa's golden palace and her choice to remain in the *Aśokavana* signifies the first step that man has to take to rise from his fallen state. Having fallen a prey to the enchantment of the senses, man ought not to indulge indiscriminately in sense gratification. He must first withdraw himself from such indulgence and perform *tapas* austerity as Sītā did. *Tapas* is an intelligent conservation and utilisation of energies towards higher pursuits in life i.e. conserving energies which are dissipated in sensual indulgences and directing such conserved energy to the goal of Self-realisation. When a man practises this he gains a relative peace and contentment which is symbolised by Sītā remaining in the *Aśokavana. Śoka* in Sanskrit means grief, *aśoka* means non-grief. With his consistent efforts towards self-control and contemplation upon the higher truth, he gains faith and confidence in his spiritual pursuits. This is symbolised by Rāma's ring that Hanumān gives to Sītā, which gives her the assurance of Rāma's arrival. Hanumān represents that strength and faith born in a spiritual man.

After his meeting with Sītā, Hanumān set fire to the whole of Laṅkā. He left behind a blazing red city to warn Rāvana of the might and glory of Rāma. Laṅkā represents material splendour. The burning of Laṅkā indicates that material splendour has no value to one who is spiritually evolved. As man advances spiritually the sense-objects of the world no longer allure him. They lose their power of enchantment. They are burnt as it were.

Vibhīṣaṇa, the younger brother of Rāvaṇa, pleaded with Rāvaṇa to give up his vicious deeds and return Sītā to Rāma. Rāvaṇa was far too proud and lustful to heed his brother's advice. The three brothers — Vibhīṣaṇa, Rāvaṇa, Kumbhakarṇa — in fact represent respectively the three *guṇas*, the mental qualities of human beings: *sattva, rajas* and *tamas. Sattva* is the pure and noble quality of the mind. *Rajas* is passion and agitation. *Tamas* is dullness and inertia. Vibhīṣaṇa was ever-poised and pure in nature. Rāvaṇa was always riddled with passionate desires and agitations. Kumbhakarṇa was known for his inertia. He would sleep for months together at a stretch. Vibhīṣaṇa's appeal to Rāvaṇa represents the *sāttvika* nature in man directing his passionate nature to the right channels. But rarely indeed does man heed the inner appeal of his *sāttvika* nature. Rāvaṇa thus rejected Vibhīṣaṇa's advice and prepared himself and his army for facing Rāma in battle. Consequently Vibhīṣaṇa left Laṅkā and surrendered to Rāma.

On the other side, Rāma and Lakṣmaṇa with the help of Sugrīva and his monkey forces prepared themselves to cross the ocean to conquer Rāvaṇa and release Sītā from her captivity. The metaphysical explanation to these events is based on the fundamental relationship between a monkey and a thought. A 'monkey' and 'thought' are identical in some respects. The monkey forces represent the human mind. A monkey, like human thought, has two distinct qualities referred to as *asthira* and *cañcala.* Both these terms mean unstable. *Sthira* means being firm at one place. *Asthira* is not being firm i.e. moving from one place to another. *Cañcala* is movement of the body while it is stationary in one place. A monkey is *asthira* in the sense that it cannot remain in one place. It keeps jumping about all the time. That is the nature of a monkey. Even if it is tied up in one place a monkey keeps fidgeting all the time indicating its *cañcala* nature. The human mind has these two qualities as well. It keeps on jumping from thought to thought. When it is given a fixed point of contemplation even then it slips into other thoughts.

These monkeys were under the suzerainty of Vāli (the lusty king) who usurped the kingdom of his brother Sugrīva (the virtuous king). Rāma destroyed Vāli and made Sugrīva the king of the monkey forces. This is the first step that Rāma had to take to win back Sītā, to destroy evil and substitute virtue in its place. The mind at present is under the governance of lust and greed. In order to gain one's spiritual nature, the initial step to be taken is to divert the mind from lust and greed to self-control and sacrifice. A mind so prepared must surrender itself to the Supreme and put forth all its efforts to attain liberation. When man makes a concerted effort with consistency of purpose, help is showered from all sides. The ocean of delusion, the sea of likes and dislikes is crossed over. The ego with ten sense organs (Rāvaṇa) is destroyed. The individual regains his lost Self. Sītā unites once again with Rāma.

The battle was won and Śitā was brought before Rāma. She passed through the test of purity by literally going through fire. She emerged unscathed. Rāma accepted her whole-heartedly. After the union, Rāma and Sītā ruled over Ayodhyā. It was a glorious reign—Rāmarājya. This last portion signifies that an individual must be cleansed of all his *vāsanās,* desires before the dawn of Realisation. When this is accomplished man gains the ultimate realisation of the Self. He lives a life of absolute peace and bliss.

# The Four Āśramas

THERE ARE four distinct stages in man's life according to the Indian tradition. They are the following four āśramas :

1. *Brahmacarya* celibacy.
2. *Gārhasthya* household.
3. *Vānaprastha* reclusion.
4. *Sannyāsa* mendicancy.

The four *āśramas* correspond to these four stages of life.

*Brahmacaryāśrama* is the early period of life when the young boy is initiated into scriptural study. The religious master, *guru* takes him as a full-time disciple and personally imparts the sacred knowledge of Vedānta to him. The *brahmacāri* celibate observes the vow of celibacy and takes in the knowledge in a spirit of surrender and worship. The initiation is usually done between the age of six and eight years and the training imparted for about 12 years. When the boy returns after completing his studies, termed *samāvarthana,* he is fully charged with spiritual knowledge. He is well-equipped to face any situation or challenge of life and work himself up to realisation of his supreme Self.

The *brahmacāri* goes through the initiation or *upanayana* ceremony when his intellect matures. That is the time when he is able to think independently. The parents of the boy conduct this ceremony in their home. The hair on the boy's head is shaven off leaving a small tuft at the back. The sacred thread consisting of three white cotton strands is put around his neck and waist like a cross-belt. The verse from a hymn of the Ṛgveda, called *Gāyatrī mantra,* is whispered in his ear. Soon after the ceremony is over the boy is sent to the *gurukula,* a traditional institution for spīritual education from a guru. The word '*upanayana*' literally means bringing near (*upa* = near, *nayana* = bringing). The ceremony is meant to bring the disciple near the master both physically and spiritually. The disciple is guided carefully and taken gradually to the highest spiritual awakening in which his guru revels.

The shaving of the head indicates the removal of desires. When the disciple approaches the teacher he is expected to leave behind all material and sensual desires and bring with him only a few spiritual desires. They are desires to serve the master, learn from him, apply his teachings to his own life and realise his supreme Self. The hair that is removed represents the material and sensual desires while the tuft left behind symbolises a few spiritual desires that he needs to carry to his master for his ultimate Realisation.

The tying of the two ends of the sacred thread around his neck and waist signifies the boy's determination to unite his finite personality to the infinite Self that he really is. The three strands of cotton comprising the sacred thread may be taken as representing the *sāttvika, rājasika* and *tāmasika guṇas* which are the three states of mind that every man is composed of, or they could be taken as the waking, dream and deep-sleep which are the three states of consciousness that man goes through. The determination of the student indicated here is his commitment to transcending these three states of the mind or the three states of consciousness and reaching the fourth state, called *turīya* in Sanskrit, which is his supreme state of Realisation.

The second stage of life is that of the *gṛhasthyāśrama.* The *gṛhasthya* householder leads his life with his wife and children performing his obligatory duties. He fulfils his sacramental rites to ancestors and gods in submission to the spiritual authority of the *brāhmaṇas.* The husband and wife live a normal marital life — disciplined, never indulgent. Both of them find a beautiful opportunity to live a life based on "giving rather than taking" and learn to love, to serve, to sacrifice. In short, married life is an ideal field for one to develop the noble qualities necessary to lead a true religious life.

Having imbibed such qualities through a disciplined life the *gṛhastha* enters the third stage called *vānaprasthāśrama.* In this stage the married man continues his companionship with his family members but develops more mental abstinence and detachment. The *vānaprasthi* recluse gains greater spiritual maturity. He practises the art of living in a spirit of dispossession amidst his possessions. He maintains a sense of detachment in all his transactions of life. With the coming of age of his sons he even renounces worldly possessions and family life and retires to solitude for contemplation and meditation.

The last stage of life is the *sannyāsāśrama.* The *sannyāsī* mendicant is a homeless beggar-saint. He renounces the world and fully attunes himself to the pure Consciousness within him. He wears an ochre-coloured robe. Ochre is the colour of fire. His ochre robes are therefore meant to indicate that his body is burnt away and he has no right to claim anything from society. He wants nothing from the world. His life is dedicated to giving, to service, to sacrifice for the betterment of humanity.

Even though there are the above four stages of life one need not mechanically go through all the stages. Some may be qualified to skip over the stage of a householder if they have no *vāsanās,* inherent tendencies to go through marital experience. Others may lead a true life of *sañnyāsī* without having to go through a ritual of taking the ochre robes of a *sañnyāsi.* In other words, the four categories enumerated above are only meant to picturise the different stages of development of a normal human being and the necessary training needed at each stage to escalate him to the realisation of the Self.

# Yajña

*YAJÑA* is one of the oldest rituals of India, a respected tradition coming from the Vedic period. It is still observed in all parts of India particularly among the orthodox Hindus. It has a deep philosophical significance which is hardly known to the worshippers. The Hindus perform the ritual religiously more out of belief than understanding.

The ritual is based mainly on worship offered through fire. A mud or brick wall trough called *kuṇḍa* is first prepared. Firewood is placed in the *kuṇḍa* and lit by Hindu priests. The priests sit around the fire and chant prayers. A large congregation assembles for the ritual. They bring grains from their homes and deposit them in the corner of the hall where the ritual is performed. As the priests chant the prayers, each member of the congregation takes a handful of grains from the stock collected and offers it to the fire with a prayer. (Ghee, clarified butter is also used as an offering). Thus, one by one all the participants offer the entire grains to the Lord of fire. When the grains are offered to the fire in the *kuṇḍa* the flames shoot up. That is considered as a sign of blessing bestowed by the Lord upon the participants. When all the grains are burnt away along with the fuel the ash is distributed as *prasāda* gift to everyone. The participants of the ritual smear the ash on the forehead in three stripes and visit the nearest temple. That concludes the entire ritual which is called *yajña.*

Fire is worshipped in most rituals. In Hinduism, worship of *Agni* Fire-god is of great significance. The reason for fire being the symbol of worship is by virtue of it being the first of the five elements which is seen. The five elements namely space, air, fire, water and earth (in the order of grossness) constitute the entire world which is perceptible, conceivable. The Reality which transcends the world cannot be directly perceived, conceived. Therefore it becomes necessary to choose a symbol from the world. Since the world is constituted of the five elements the choice of the symbol is limited to these five. Since fire is the first to be seen it has been chosen as the appropriate symbol of the unseen. Another reason for the choice is perhaps the comforting nature of fire in the cold northern part of India where the idea originated. It was easier to associate fire with *Ātman* Reality because of its benevolent and beneficial character.

The entire yajña symbolises worship for active as well as contemplative persons. The same ritual explains how the activities of a man of action and a man of contemplation can be converted into worship in their respective fields.

A man of action is one who has many *vāsanās,* desires. He needs to get rid of them to purify his inner personality and unveil his real Self. This can be achieved by working in his field of activity without ego and egocentric desires in a spirit of surrender to a higher altar. Human activities these days are selfish and egocentric. Such activities produce more *vāsanās,* desires, agitations in an individual. To render them more spiritual, one has to direct the activities to a higher cause, a common purpose, a nobler ideal and work selflessly without looking for the fruits thereof. Then the actions are blessed with material success and mental peace.

The *kuṇḍa* represents any field of activity in this world. The offering of grains to the *kuṇḍa* symbolises the offering of each one's faculties in one's field of activity. Each one performs one's activity in a spirit of surrender to a higher cause instead of entertaining a selfish motive. This attitude converts selfish action into a spiritual action. The result is that his *vāsanās,* desires are destroyed and that is indicated by the consummation of the fuel in the *kuṇḍa. Vāsanās,* desires are of three distinct types namely *sāttvika, rājasika* and *tāmasika.* The smearing of the ash on the forehead is meant to declare that the individual has transcended all the three types of *vāsanās.* Entering the temple thereafter signifies that he has merged with the God-consciousness. He has realised the supreme Self.

The same ritual also symbolises how a man of contemplation worships in this world. A man of contemplation is spiritually more advanced than a man of action by virtue of a reduction of *vāsanās,* desires. When desires are reduced man becomes less active, more contemplative. In other words, his organs of action, *karmendriyas* do not function as much as his organs of perception, *jñānendriyas.* Owing to the lack of desires his reactions and responses to the external stimuli are reduced to the minimum. He merely perceives the world. The *yajña* explains how such a person can convert mere perception into spiritual practice. How an introverted person can worship through perceptions alone. The *kuṇḍa* in this case represents his physical body. The fire element in the *kuṇḍa* stands for the supreme Self. The *paṇḍits* priests sitting around the fire represent his sense organs. When the stimuli from the external world — colour and form for the eyes, sound for the ears, taste for the tongue, smell for the nose and touch for the skin — reach him he sees, hears, tastes, smells and feels respectively. In being conscious of various perceptions, his mind is directed to the presence of the pure Consciousness, *Ātman* within him. In every perception he becomes aware of the Consciousness which is responsible for his perceptions. Stimuli are like *āhuti* offerings; perceptions are like the flames glowing. Thus every perception becomes a worship. Worship is a full-time awareness of the Reality, not a part-time ritual. The *yajña* should go on all the time through action and perception. That alone would take you to Godhood.

# Temple

INDIA is a land of temples. The Hindu temple is a house of worship like any other but it has certain unique features which elevate it to great spiritual merit and recognition. The orthodox Hindu temple is symbolically designed. Its location, construction and rituals are of special significance. They are all designed to indicate the path that man has to take to evolve himself spiritually and reach the goal of Self-realisation.

The main temples in India are situated on top of the hills. The paths to these temples were narrow and rugged. The pilgrims had to walk up the hill in single file. They had to brave the many exigencies and difficulties of the jungle path before they could reach the shrine. They carried with them fruits and flowers to offer to the Lord in the temple. All these are significant.

The location of the temple at a high altitude signifies that spiritual evolution is above all mundane achievements in this world and to gain spiritual perfection one needs to put in a great deal of self-effort. The seeker has to be single-pointed and consistent in his efforts and overcome the many temptations and challenges that confront him in his spiritual path. The single file footpath to the temples indicates that the seeker of truth is all alone in his spiritual pursuit. He cannot share it with anyone. He may seek the help of his *guru* and other associates but ultimately he has to proceed all by himself in his journey to truth.

Today there are broad asphalted roads and fast transport systems to reach the same temples. People visit them in groups making a picnic out of a pilgrimage. The purpose of the age-old spiritual practice has been lost.

Fruit is taken by a spiritual seeker and offered to the temple or to his *guru*. The priest in the temple or *guru* receives it from the seeker. In such long journeys the ideal fruit that would stay fresh without decaying is the coconut.

A fruit is the product of a tree. It is the result, the effect produced. Similarly, the result or product of all past *karmas* activities of man is his present *vāsanās,* desires. When *vāsanās,* desires are removed from a person he gains Godhood.

Man minus *vāsanās*/desires = God.

Both fruit and *vāsanās* are similar in the sense that they are end products. A fruit is chosen to represent the *vāsanās,* desires of man. When a devotee offers a fruit to the Lord it signifies the offering of his *vāsanās,* desires and thereby unfolding his inner Self. His visit to the temple therefore symbolises exhaustion of his *vāsanās,* desires and realisation of his Self.

The coconut is the most popular offering in the temples of India. Besides the fact that the coconut stays fresh for many days its choice for the offering has a deeper significance. The coconut has a smooth skin on the outside while its inside is all coarse, knotted up with coir. The coir grows out of the hard shell. Within the hard shell is the kernel. The seeker removes the coir from the shell leaving a small tuft on one side and offers the full coconut to the priest. The priest breaks the shell and tears the tuft of coir away exposing three black spots on the shell. The pure white kernel is then exposed. The prayers are chanted and the coconut is offered to the deity.

The smooth outer skin of the coconut represents man's gross physical body. Within the gross body is the subtle body consisting of desires and attachments. The coir matted together represents man's entanglement with desires and attachments in this world. These desires and attachments arise from his causal body which again is represented by the hard shell.

When a seeker goes to a temple or *guru* he leaves all his worldly desires and attachments except those that are necessary for his spiritual evolution. These few desires left in him solely for his spiritual pursuit are symbolised by the small tuft of coir. The removal of the tuft means the exhaustion of the last traces of desires in the seeker. The breaking of the shell is the transcendence of the causal body and the exposure of the kernel is realisation of the supreme Self.

The flowers offered in a temple also represent *vāsānas.* Each flower is a *vāsanā.* The ritual of flower offerings is to be done in a particular way. The devotee uses the five fingers of the right hand to pick up a flower gently, then turns the fingers with the flower upwards and softly offers the flower at the Lord's feet. This ritual is performed repeatedly until all the flowers are offered. The Lord's feet represent the supreme Reality. Feet are the substratum upon which the personality rests. They represent the foundation of one's personality. That foundation is the Reality. So offering the flowers signifies giving up your *vāsanās* or desires and merging with the Reality. This is indicated by the ritual. The five fingers are directed towards the ground to pick up a flower. The fingers represent the five senses. When man's five senses are drawn towards the mundane world they pick up a *vāsanā*. But when the senses are directed towards the higher Self, represented by the fingers turning upwards the *vāsanās* get eliminated. When this practice is maintained consistently all the *vāsanās* get exhausted and man becomes one with God.

The devotee prostrates himself before his *guru* or in the temple. He lies flat on his stomach with arms stretched over his head and his palms together. His head, intellect and his heart, mind are in line with the Lord's feet, Reality. This signifies that his entire personality has merged with God.

Again, the very construction of the temple indicates the path to Self-realisation. The idol is in the sanctum sanctorum, a dark room where there is a small oil lamp burning perpetually. Around the sanctum sanctorum is a closed passage on all four sides. Outside this is a wider passage with the roof covered. Beyond the walls of this is a still broader passage without a roof over it. The entrance to the temple leads to this wide open passage. Thus there are three passages enveloping the shrine. The three passages leading to the sanctum sanctorum refer to the gross, subtle and causal bodies of man. Within his three bodies lies the supreme Self which is unknown, dark to him. If man wants to reach his inner Self he must cross the limitations of his gross, subtle and causal bodies and seek within. The outermost passage of the temple which is open to the sky indicates the gross body which deals with the outer world. Man identifies himself with his gross body and gets involved in the external world. To regain his spiritual Self he must first rise above worldly entanglements and delve deeper into his personality. When he does that he enters the realm of his subtle body consisting of his desires and thoughts. That is indicated by the devotee moving to the next passage in the temple with the closed roof. Remaining there again is spiritual stagnation. He must rise above desires and thoughts and move on to the next passage, the causal body, and transcend it. The causal body is his *vāsanās* which is the seat of ignorance. He must get rid of his *vāsanās* through spiritual knowledge before he can come in contact with his real Self, the *Ātman* represented by the shrine.

The devotee reaches the sanctum sanctorum. It is all dark. The idol is not seen. The oil lamp burning indicates that the *Ātman* is the everlasting light of wisdom. Man can use it at any time to destroy his ignorance and regain the knowledge of his Self. The priest lights a piece of camphor from this oil lamp and shows it to the idol. As the camphor burns the smoke escapes and the image brightens. The devotee has his *darśana*—vision of the Lord.

The burning of the camphor is again significant. Camphor is in a solid form. But when a pure sample of camphor is left exposed for a period of time it sublimates into mere fragrance leaving no solid substance behind. It is most aptly suited to represent the human personality. For man is nothing but his *vāsanās* in a substantial form. *Vāsanās* themselves are the insubstantial, inconceivable, inexpressible essence of the human personality. They determine the individual nature. They give out his personal fragrance as it were. When *vāsanās* are eliminated what remains is his pure Self, the *Ātman.*

*Ātman* plus *vāsanās* = human being.
Human being minus *vāsanās* = *Ātman.*

This is achieved by taking the light of wisdom from the altar of the Self. When *vāsanās* ignorance are destroyed by knowledge, the ego vanishes and man realises his supreme Self.

*Prasāda* gift of food is distributed after the *darśana* vision of the Lord. *Prasāda* in Sanskrit literally means calmness, equanimity. The distribution of *prasāda* therefore signifies the attainment of the supreme bliss of Realisation, the bliss of the Self that man gains when he transcends the limitations of his gross, subtle and causal bodies.

### *THE EROTIC SCULPTURES AT KHAJURĀHO AND KONĀRAK*

Some of the temples in India have erotic sculptures. Khajurāho and Konārak are particularly known for them. These sculptures have been severely criticised. Some explanations are offered which do not really satisfy the critics. The rationale of temple architecture has not been adequately projected. A deeper study and analysis reveals the pristine elegance of the ancient ideas embedded in them.

The human mind is ever preoccupied with acquisition of material objects and enjoyment of sensual pleasures of the terrestrial world. Its attention is hardly directed to the transcendental Being. All our senses are constantly gorged by us at the cost of sensibility. With an idea of turning the mind introvert, the ancient Hindu sages divinised practically everything in this world. By doing so they were successful in reminding the mind of the Supreme several times a day even as it was engaged in the desired objects of the world. For instance, Hinduism has personified wealth and riches in the form of Goddess Laksmī. So a man who runs after material wealth is made to remember the goddess in all his transactions. Thus there is a touch of divinity in his material pursuits. Another man pursues knowledge which is personified as Goddess Sarasvatī. So his mind is also drawn to the higher, even as he is engaged in the pursuit of wordly knowledge. Thus there are numerous gods covering the entire sphere of human activities.

The life of a Hindu is a series of prayer and worship. Everything is divinised from the cradle to the grave. There is a ritual associated with every aspect of the Hindu life. The entire passage from birth to death is nothing but a series of rituals and religious ceremonies, prayer and worship. The idea is to remind his dissipating mind constantly of the purpose of his existence in the world which is to unfold the Self, to realise his Godhood.

Sex and procreative functions have also been treated as a divine aspect of human life. In the olden days, it was a common practice for parents to take their children to temples every evening at dusk. As the parents approached the sanctum sanctorum the bells and cymbals, chants and prayers, the incense and *āratī* sacred flame were all pitched up to the highest devotion. At that time the children, immature as they were, strolled around looking at the different sculptures. They noticed the sensual carvings but did not understand what they meant. But as the children grew up, the sensual presentation and the devotional ecstasy synchronised due to constant association of the two ideas. Later when as adults they took to wedlock, the procreative function was automatically treated with spiritual beauty and serenity. It was a scientific system to educate children about the realities of life.

# Śiva Liṅga

THE INFINITE REALITY is beyond the reach of the finite equipments of man. Reality cannot be experienced through *pratyakṣa* direct perception. The scriptures therefore rely mainly on two sources of knowledge, namely *anumāna* inference and *upamā* comparison, for expressing the inexpressible Reality. Śiva Liṅga is one such indirect means of communicating the Reality.

*Liṅga* in Sanskrit means symbol. Śiva Liṅga is a symbol of Śiva. Śiva in this context refers to the infinite Reality. Symbolism is an art of representing thoughts and ideas, objectives and ideals etc. through the medium of signs or symbols. Symbolism is not a science to be investigated. A symbol merely takes one to the thing symbolised by virtue of some similarity between the two. Hindu symbolism explains the Truth of religion and philosophy through idols and forms, signs and stories. All Hindu symbols have spiritual significance relating to life. The study of symbolism lies in proper and faithful interpretations of the relationship which exists between the Reality and the form symbolising the Reality.

The Dravidians originated the Śiva Liṅga as a symbol of the supreme Reality. The Narmadā river contained marble-like stones shaped beautifully in the form of an ellipsoid by the running waters. An ellipsoid is shaped like an elongated sphere having two foci instead of one as in the case of a sphere. The ellipsoid represents *Śiva-śakti.* The two foci of the ellipsoid correspond to the two aspects of the Reality: *Śiva* the immanent, *śakti* the manifest.

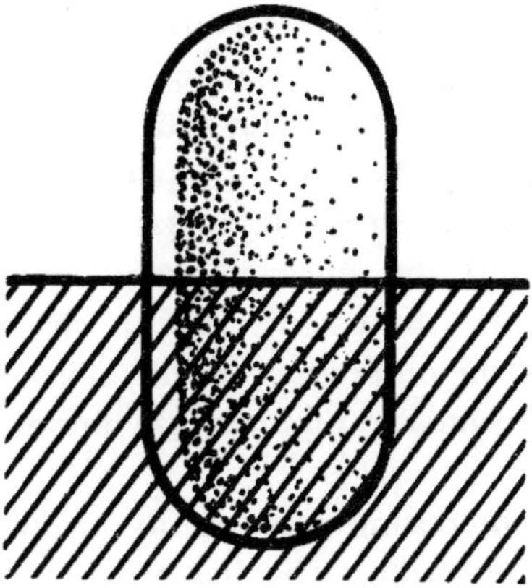

The Śiva Liṅga ellipsoid is fixed in such a way that one half of it lies embedded in the earth while the other half remains outside the surface. The upper half that appears above the surface represents the seen, visible manifest world of plurality, *śakti.* The lower half under the surface is the unseen invisible substratum, the supporter of the upper half. That rightly represents the unmanifest supreme Reality, *Śiva.* The properties of the ellipsoid are ideally suited for symbolising the two aspects of the Reality — the unmanifest and manifest.

A cross-section of the ellipsoid cut along its axis is an ellipse whereas its cross-section cut at right angles to its axis is a circle. The ellipsoid thus is a combination of ellipses and circles. The circle represents the supreme Reality. A circle has no beginning or end. The Reality also has no beginning or end. One part of an ellipsoid, namely the circle, therefore represents the unmanifest Reality. The other part which is the ellipse represents the manifest universe. The entire universe consisting of an atom right upto the solar system is in a way related to the ellipse. The solar system consists of the sun with the planets revolving around it. The motion of each planet around the sun describes an ellipse. Strikingly similar is the motion of the electrons around the nucleus in an atom. The orbits described by the movements of the electrons are also ellipses. Hence the other aspect of the ellipsoid, namely the ellipse, is most suited to represent the universe.

Another interesting reference to the Śiva Liṅga is that it represents the phallus. This has provoked criticism both from the West and the East. The critics feel that this idea has reduced the Hindu ritual and worship to absurdity. Whether the *liṅga* was originally meant to represent the phallus is difficult to establish authoritatively. Nevertheless, a subtle inner meaning could be read in the seemingly absurd symbolism.

Lord Śiva represents the power of destruction while Lord Brahmā and Viṣṇu represent the power of creation and maintenance respectively. These three powers are the manifestation of the supreme Reality in this world. In fact, these three powers are inseparable. In other words, they are only three facets of the same power. There can be no creation without destruction. Nor destruction without creation. For example, when the morning is dead noon is born, when noon is dead evening is born, when evening is dead night is born and so on. In this chain of births and deaths, creation and destruction, the day is maintained. Thus, the third power namely the power of maintenance also is ingrained in the other two powers of creation and destruction. To indicate this inseparable nature of creation and destruction Śiva, the Lord of destruction, has been represented by the organ of procreation.

# The Bull and the Cow

THE HINDUS consider the bull and the cow as sacred. This has a significance. The worship of these animals means worshipping the principle of sacrifice and service which they represent so that the worshippers could imbibe this great principle into their own living. Today the basis of worship is lost, the principle of sacrifice and service is hardly practised by anyone although the orthodox Hindus hold on to these animals fanatically.

The bull is called Nandī. A stone carving of Nandī is seen in the Śiva temple outside the sanctum sanctorum with its head turned towards the shrine. The idol and its positioning carry a meaning. India being basically an agricultural country, the bull plays a very important role in the lives of people. Even after the innovation of tractors in the agricultural fields, the bull is indispensable. Besides its utility in the agricultural fields the bull also epitomises the very culture of India. It demonstrates a great principle of living. The bull toils the whole day in the hot sun and helps cultivate the fields for producing grains throughout the length and breadth of India. In return for its hard labour it gets only some dry grass and water for its sustenance. It seems to function on the principle "Maximum work minimum profit." There is no ego or egocentric desires polluting its work. No *kartṛtva bhāvanā* doership or *bhoktṛtva bhāvanā* enjoyership attitude at all. Its activities are not driven by any desires. Neither does it crave for the fruits of its actions. It plays its role without worries of the past and anxieties of the future. It merely does what it ought to do in life. That is the highest principle of action, the best code of living. The ancient Hindus recognised this lofty principle in the life of a bull. They tried to emulate it in all their activities. They invoked the sacrificial spirit of the bull in their own lives. They worshipped the bull.

The head of the bull is turned towards the shrine in the temple. This indicates that the bull's actions are dedicated to God, an absence of ego and egocentric desires. By worshipping the bull, the Hindu invokes its spirit of dedication to higher values and service to fellow-beings. That is the spirit of *karma yoga,* the path of action.

Lord Kṛṣṇa refers to Arjuna in the Bhagavad Gītā as a *Bharataṛṣabha.* It literally means 'bull among the *Bhāratas*'. Today people all over the world seem to follow the principle of "minimum work maximum profit". There is a need to change the basic attitude towards work, to imbibe the spirit of sacrifice and service, to graft the principle of "maximum work minimum profit" in their day-to-day living. To be a bull in society! That is the advice given by Kṛṣṇa.

The cow is also considered a sacred animal, revered and worshipped by Hindus. Again, you find in the cow a spirit of true sacrifice and service. The cow also follows the great principle of life based on the attitude of giving. It gives wholesome milk to the society. Milk is a universal food consumed by one and all: the new-born, child, youth, middle-aged, old, invalid and healthy. The cow gives something valuable to society and takes hardly anything in return.

The cow-worshippers are only trying to imbibe this great quality the attitude of 'giving' into their own lives. If the attitude of 'taking' prevails in a society its members develop selfish demands and desires. Consequently there is struggle, stress and strain in that society. Let their attitude change to giving, their demands and desires drop their selfishness. Harmony, peace and happiness reign in that very same society. The dignity of the human race is founded on the principle of giving. Victor Hugo summarizes an ideal life in one simple sentence: Life is to give, not to take. The ancient Hindus tried to instil this high principle in their own lives. For this reason the cow was considered sacred. Unfortunately this principle is lost and people worship the body of the cow fanatically.

A fuller understanding of the lofty principles the cow and the bull live by would usher humanity to a more meaningful, purposeful life.

# Tilaka and Namaskāra

TILAKA is the mark of red powder or sandalwood paste that is applied on the forehead. It is used by the Hindus. It has become practically a symbol of Hinduism.

To a Hindu the daily bath carries a lot of sanctity. It is a part of his prayer and worship. Immediately after bath the Hindu performs his daily prayer usually in his temple or in his own house. After his prayer is over, he takes a little red or sandal powder or sacred ash placed at the feet of the Lord and applies it to his forehead. The ladies usually make a round mark and that is called *tilaka.* Men are more accustomed to use it in the form of a straight line. Whatever way these marks are made the Hindu retains it through the day.

This practice has a significance. The Hindu believes that the purpose of life is to realise the infinite Reality. This is achieved by reflection and contemplation which he practises in his prayer-room. But he cannot continue his prayer all day long since his duties and obligations compel him to go into the world and work. He therefore leaves his prayer room with the idea of coming back to it after fulfilling his obligations. While leaving he takes a little powder from the Lord and applies it to his forehead, with an idea to remember that all his actions in the external world are dedicated to the achievement of this supreme

Goal of Realisation. The forehead is the seat of memory. Applying the *tilaka* on the forehead symbolises the retention of the memory of the Lord in all his activities. That is to remember, to reflect and contemplate upon the Reality in and through his activities throughout the day.

When a Hindu meets another Hindu the first thing that strikes them both is the mark on the forehead. It constantly reminds each other of the purpose of their existence, their dedication to the realisation of the supreme Reality. They confirm this understanding by greeting each other with folded arms. This gesture is called *namaskāra.* The gesture of *namaskāra* is to join the two palms together in front of him and bow his head to the joint palms.

Each palm represents the separate individuality. Each palm supports the five fingers. Similarly, each personality has five sheaths called the five *kośas.* The five different parts of the personality are called *pañcakośas,* five sheaths. They are: *annamayakośa* food sheath, *prāṇamayakośa* vital-air sheath *manomayakośa* mental sheath, *vijñānamayakośa* intellectual sheath and *ānandamayakośa* bliss sheath. These five sheaths are supported by the *Ātman,* the supreme Self which is the eternal Reality. The five sheaths are different from individual to individual but the Reality that supports them all is one and the same in all individualities. This truth is declared when the Hindus greet each other with *namaskāra.* The two palms joined together as one indicates that the Reality or *Ātman* in both is one and the same. To this unifying Infinite *Ātman* the Hindu bows in reverence when he does *namaskāra.*

# Festivals

## *DIVĀLĪ OR DĪPĀVALĪ*

INDIA is a land of festivals. Divālī is the festival of lights, a festival of the Hindus traced back to ancient times. It is the most gorgeous festival celebrated all over the country.

'Divālī' is derived from 'Dīpāvalī' meaning 'a cluster of lights'. The celebration of Divālī is marked by illumination everywhere. Rows and rows of small earthernware lamps are seen in every home. Divālī is also known for fireworks which go on practically the whole night. In every house the children, even elders, light fire crackers. That night sounds like a battle-field everywhere.

Early next morning before sunrise, every member of the family takes the holy bath and wears new clothes. From the poorest to the richest Indian, wearing new clothes is an established ritual. Thereafter all of them visit relatives and friends where gifts are exchanged and sweets consumed with much gaiety.

Divālī, or more correctly Dīpāvalī, is a joyous celebration of the death of the Titan of hell, Narakāsura at the hands of Lord Kṛṣṇa. Narakāsura, known as the son of the earth, was all-powerful. He was an intolerable menace to the gods, sages and all men of piety. He looted and plundered not only the earth but heaven as well. He carried away 16,000 fair daughters of the gods and imprisoned them in his harem. The gods led by Indra approached Lord Kṛṣṇa and supplicated the Lord to destroy the demon. Kṛṣṇa readily agreed. He fought a fierce battle. After destroying thousands of demons Kṛṣṇa slew Narakāsura. Thereafter he rescued the imprisoned damsels and at their earnest prayers took them as his wives.

This festival, like all other festivals and rituals, explains the inner personality of man and his deliverance from his ignorance and ego to attainment of his supreme nature of God-realisation. The darkness of the night represents man's total ignorance of his Self, ignorance of his Godhood. In that darkness reigns the desire-ridden ego which destroys peace and brings about sorrow and misery in the bosom of man. The 16,000 damsels represent the desires that arise in an egoistic man. Desires dwell in ignorance under the control of the ego. All these desires cannot find fulfilment in this limited world. They remain frustrated. Thus man is driven to a state of sorrow and suffering by his own negative tendencies.

To pull himself out of this state man has to employ his positive tendencies to direct his attention to the higher Self. Every man has within him both positive and negative tendencies. They have been represented in almost all religions as gods and demons respectively. The gods' approach of Kṛṣṇa for help signifies man's positive tendencies reaching for the Self. When man turns introvert and seeks the inner Self his negative tendencies get destroyed one by one. His desires get annihilated. This is represented by the fireworks on the night of Divālī. The battle with the ego, the fight with the negative tendencies, the destruction of the desires goes on the whole night, that is as long as ignorance lasts. With the rising of the sun all darkness is dispelled, all ignorance removed, all desires destroyed. Ego, the Narakāsura, is killed. Man is transformed to his original Godhead.

The bath at the dawn of Divālī indicates the cleansing of the egoborn, egocentric desires. The new clothes signify the newly acquired Godhood. That transformation brings about gaiety, joy, bliss represented by eating sweets and merry-making. The visiting of relatives and friends the next morning carries this new vision, the vision of Divinity, the vision of the supreme Self in one and all.

*DASSEHRĀ OR VIJAYĀDAŚAMĪ*

*DASSEHRĀ* is another popular festival of India. The festival lasts for ten days beginning on the first day of the Hindu month of *Aśvin* (September/October). It is celebrated in various ways all over the country. It is observed as Durgā-pūjā, as Vijayādaśamī celebrating the victory of Lord Rāma over Rāvaṇa, as Navarātri or the festival of nine nights.

The goddess Durgā was created by the three gods — Brahmā, Viṣṇu, Maheśvara — for destroying the *dasyūs* demons. The demons sent their most powerful representative Mahiṣāsura in the form of a buffalo to fight Durgā. The goddess fought with this great demon and killed him. The buffalo represents the lower animal instincts in man in an aggressive form. The goddess represents the higher, nobler tendencies also in an aggressive form — the form of Durgā.

Man is a mere expression of his inner nature. Man's inner nature falls under two broad classifications. You may call them the aggressive and the passive. Again each of these is of two types depending on their qualities of goodness or badness. Thus there are four distinct natures covering the entire range of inner personalities of human beings.

A passive man is one who functions according to the fancies of his mind without the intervention of his intellect. He follows a routine, mechanical, traditional pattern of life. His actions emanate from his feelings and emotions rather than his discrimination. He does not question the merit or demerit of his actions. He lives blindly the life set by his predecessors and ancestors. Environment and circumstances shape his individuality instead of his individuality shaping them. In short, he lives an unintelligent dogged life of passive acceptance of whatever he encounters in the world. He has neither the initiative nor the enthusiasm to utilise his resources intelligently for a more meaningful and purposeful life.

Passivity in man may lean towards good or bad. A passively bad man is one who is involved in wrong, immoral activities but does not intend to be so. He does not wilfully and cunningly plan or scheme activities to meet his private ends. He does not mean to be bad. He merely continues a wrong way of life usually inherited from his past. His intellect does not consciously analyse and supervise his activities or their repercussions. He is caught up in a mode of living which happens to be bad. So it is with a passively good man. A passively good man is involved in a way of life which happens to be moral and benevolent. He may not realise his activities to be good. He merely executes his good impulses. He does not intend to be virtuous. A passively good man also does not intellectually analyse and supervise his activities or their consequences. Such unintelligent benevolence at times proves detrimental to his community and himself.

The aggressive nature of man's personality is distinct and different from his passivity. Contrary to the passively bad, an aggressively bad man is one who intends to be bad. He wilfully and viciously plans and schemes, manipulates and manoeuvres corrupt and immoral ways of life for meeting his own selfish ends. He has no scruples to follow. He breaks customs, tradition, rules and regulations to get things done to satisfy his ego and egocentric desires. The aggressive are more powerful; they dominate over the passive good and bad. The simple reason for their superiority is that they employ their intellect whereas the passive use only their mind in their activities.

An aggressively good person is one whose basic nature is good. He also uses his power of discrimination all the time to decide the type of activities that he executes. He does not act impulsively. He studies facts, foresees consequences, reasons carefully and acts in the best interests of all. At times the actions of the aggressively good may appear *prima facie* bad but they are benevolent to the core. They may be 'cruel only to be kind'. Even a single aggressively good person present in a community can bring about peace, prosperity and happiness to all its people.

The proportion of passive individuals in any society far exceeds the aggressive. Most human beings are content to lead a routine, stereotyped life. They do not care to exert and strive to achieve anything beyond a mechanical existence. The aggressive ones who utilise their superior power of reason and reflection are fewer in number. Even among the aggressive the percentage of the good is small.

The law pertaining to the inner personalities of human beings holds good universally. The layman is not even aware of its existence, much less does he understand how it functions. Consequently, he does not make use of the law in practical living. He becomes frustrated in life. He complains bitterly that the world is polluted, that honesty does not pay these days. Why do the good and honest have to suffer at the hands of the bad and dishonest? — that is his question. The problem is easily answered in the light of the above analysis of human nature. The vast majority of human beings are passive. The aggressive bad prey on the passive good and bad. They intelligently calculate and manipulate things to benefit themselves at the expense of others. The passive ones are naturally the victims of such vicious practices. The passive continue to be passive. They merely mumble and grumble at the success of the aggressive. The only solution to the problem is for them to shed their inertia and operate with their intellects. They must appreciate the working of the law of human nature. Remaining in their mental and emotional plane, they cannot combat those who operate from a higher level of human personality. They must employ their available intellectual faculties and seek, if necessary, intellectual guidance from superiors to combat the viciousness of the aggressive bad. Thus the passive have to turn to aggressive goodness to be able to fight and conquer the aggressive bad elements in society. There is no other way to do it.

A classic example of passive goodness is depicted in the character of Yudhiṣṭhira, the eldest brother of the Pāṇḍava princes in the epic Mahābhārata. Yudhiṣṭhira was an embodiment of goodness. But his goodness rose largely from his emotional personality. Consequently his brothers, wife and he suffered untold humiliation and excruciation at the hands of his royal cousin, the Kaurava prince Duryodhana. Duryodhana was a perfect specimen of aggressive badness. He schemed and planned the destruction of his passively good cousins. In this context the epic shows how aggressive goodness, the supreme of all human natures, combats and wins over aggressive badness. Lord Kṛṣṇa was a picture of aggressive goodness. Kṛṣṇa employed his goodness intelligently to destroy the aggressively bad Kauravas and relieve the suffering of the Pāṇḍavas. Thus even a single aggressively good individual can resurrect the righteousness of a country lost to the evil doings of the aggressive bad.

The victory of Durgā is the triumph of the aggressive good over evil, the destruction of *vāsanās,* desires and realisation of the divine Self.

Even Rāma is said to have performed Durgā-pujā and invoked the blessings of the goddess before he left for

Laṅkā to fight Rāvaṇa. Rāma killed Rāvaṇa and regained Sītā. This story again represents the destruction of evil (Rāvaṇa) and the reunion with the supreme Self (Rāma).

The nine days' worship is divided into three days' worship for each of the three goddesses — Durgā, the goddess of protection and valour, Lakṣmī, the goddess of wealth and Sarasvatī, the goddess of knowledge. The tenth day, Vijayadaśamī is the day of victory when huge effigies of the demon Rāvaṇa are burnt with fireworks. This is followed by feasting, entertainment and rejoicing.

The effigies represent the ego. The fireworks is the battle with the ego. When the *vāsanās* are all destroyed, the Self, the *Ātman* is realised. The worship of Durgā for the first three days of the festival signifies the destruction of negative *vāsanās*/tendencies inherent in man like jealousy, greed, passion etc. The next three days' worship of Lakṣmī signifies the establishment of positive tendencies like affection, charity, forgiveness etc. The last three days dedicated to Sarasvatī is the gaining of knowledge of the supreme Self. Three days are allotted to each goddess to indicate the discipline and training to be practised at the three levels of the personality, namely physical, mental and intellectual, to achieve the goal set for each type of worship. The nine days of spiritual discipline and training are only symbolic. It is not to be considered as the time required for a man to achieve spiritual unfoldment. The victorious tenth day — Vijayadaśamī — represents the day of enlightenment when all *vāsanās* are destroyed and the knowledge of the Self has dawned in the individual. The individual is said to have attained God-realisation.

# PART III
## Invocations and Prayers

# The Symbol ॐ (Om)

ॐ, pronounced Om, is a symbol of the supreme *Brahman.* Om is an 'idol' representing the divine ideal. It is considered the most powerful word-symbol used for meditation. *Brahman* is the ultimate Reality sought by all spiritual practitioners. It cannot be reached directly through human equipment. *Brahman* is not something you can perceive with your sense organs. Nor is it an emotion that you can feel with your mind. Nor a concept you can comprehend with your intellect. *Brahman* is the ideal unknown to you. You need a known idol to reach the unknown ideal. An idol takes you to the ideal. The idol can be either gross or subtle. An example of a gross idol is the stone image in a temple. Fire is a subtler idol. Sound is the subtlest of all idols. It is considered subtlest because only one of the five sense organs viz. the ear can contact it. Of all sounds Om is the most potent, natural. There are reasons for the choice of Om :

(i) Sounds are of two kinds — articulate and inarticulate. Articulate sound is that which can be represented by letters of the alphabet. The articulate or alphabetical sound is concerned with topics which deal with the knowledge of the head. The other type of sound is the inarticulate or intonational. The inarticulate or intonational sound deals with the heart. Articulate sound has a limited application. It is understood only by people who have learnt it through training. A man comes and speaks to you in Persian or Russian. You do not understand him. You have not undergone that training. He does not know your language either. Nevertheless when he begins to laugh you understand him. You know that he is happy. Suppose you begin to cry. He understands you are unhappy. This language is inarticulate. It is intonational, a universal language uttered and understood by even babies and animals. Music is another example of intonation. The sound of music has a marvellous effect. It produces wonderful results. The word Om has the advantages of both the articulate and inarticulate, alphabetical and intonational. It has a deep philosophical significance. You will appreciate it when you learn its meaning. Besides, the chant of Om has an extraordinary effect on human beings. It produces harmony, peace and bliss to one and all. Om brings the individual being in perfect attunement with the eternal being.

(ii) The proper way to write Om is A-U-M, अ-उ-म् in Sanskrit. According to Sanskrit grammar अ (A) and उ (U) when connected together coalesce into ओ (O). Even the mute can produce the sounds of A-U-M. अ (A) is the sound emanating from the base of the throat. उ (U) is the sound produced by the impulse rolling forward in the mouth. म् (M) is the sound produced by closing the lips. There is no sound beyond these two extremities viz. throat and lips. So Om covers the full range of sounds. It represents the entire phenomenon of sound.

(iii) The symbol ॐ (Om) stands for the pure Consciousness which pervades the three states of waking, dream and deep-sleep. It is also called *praṇava. Praṇava* means something that pervades life or runs through *prāṇa* or breath. The sound अ (pronounced uh), according to Vedānta, represents the material world, all that is observed in the wakeful state of consciousness. The second sound उ (pronounced oo) represents all the experience of the dreamland, the subject and objects of the dreaming state of consciousness. म् (pronounced im) represents all the unknown in the deep-sleep state of consciousness. While chanting Om you will have to concentrate your attention and put forth feeling in realising that your *Ātman*, your Self is the stern Reality pervading the three worlds.

(iv) Om is the real name of the Almighty. It is the key that unlocks the kingdom of heaven. This mantra does not belong to any particular language. The Hindus took it up. It does not mean that it belongs to the Hindus. It is a natural syllable. It is nature's word, nature's *mantra.* It is the name of god. Some people discard it because they believe it comes from Sanskṛit, from the Hindus. They reject it on the ground that it is not their special label. The word Om is not subjected to the same conjugation or reflection or other grammatical manipulations to which all other Sanskṛit words are subjected. So it is not a Sanskṛit word. It is a word of nature, a pure and genuine word by itself. The Hindus made good use of it. So can you. Om occupies a very prominent place in all languages of the world. Omniscient, omnipotent, omnipresent are the highest names for god. They begin with Om. In your prayers when you reach the point of silence you utter Om in some form or other. In English you end the prayer with Amen. In Arabic, Persian and Hindustani you say Amīn.

In meditation the mind keeps chanting the *mantra* Om. The momentary silence that exists between every two successive chants is called *amātrā*. *Amātrā* represents the pure Consciousness, the *Ātman*. In the final stage of meditation your mind is held in single-pointed chant. The function of the intellect is discrimination between pairs of opposites. Your intellect is engaged in discriminating between Om and *amātrā*. In the peak of meditation you must stop the chant. What follows is absolute Silence. There is no more sound of Om. No thought. With the extinction of the last thought your mind is extinct. There is no longer the pair of sound and silence. In the absence of a pair no discrimination is possible. Without discrimination your intellect is extinct as well. Your mind and intellect are thus transcended in that absolute Silence. That is the sacred moment of Realisation. Your individual self merges with the infinite Self.

# Invocations

# I

## गीता ध्यानम्
## Gītā Dhyānam

## ध्यान श्लोका:
## Dhyāna Ślokās

The Dhyāna Ślokās are an invocatory prayer to the Bhagavad Gītā. They are nine verses attributed to Madhusūdana Sarasvatī. Preceptor and disciple follow a traditional practice to chant the invocation before commencing the study of the Gītā. The chant helps the disciple attune his mind and intellect to understand the deep import of the Gītā.

The mind and intellect are caught up in perception, emotion and thought of the ever-changing material world. Right through life the individual is lost in terrestrial affairs. His thoughts seldom rise to the transcendental Reality. The mind and intellect needs to be prepared for receiving the philosophy of the Bhagavad Gītā. The invocatory prayer serves this purpose. It shifts the focus of attention from the world to God. The chant attunes the seeker to the subtle theme of the scripture.

The first verse of the Dhyāna Ślokās eulogises the text, Śrīmad Bhagavad Gītā. Worships the sacred book as mother Gītā. The second verse pays homage to the author, sage Vyāsa. The third and fourth surrender in devotion to Lord Kṛṣṇa, the guru in the book. The next three verses subtly refer to the three spiritual disciplines of *karma* action, *bhakti* devotion and *jñānam* knowledge. The eighth indicates the high spiritual state the seeker reaches as a result of following the discipline. He then becomes qualified for contemplation and meditation. The concluding verse takes him to single-pointed meditation and realisation of the supreme Self.

Verse 1

ॐ पार्थाय प्रतिबोधितां भगवता नारायणेन स्वयम्
व्यासेन ग्रथितां पुराणमुनिना मध्येमहाभारतम्।
अद्वैतामृतवर्षिणीं भगवतीमष्टादशाध्यायिनीम्
अम्ब त्वामनुसन्दधामि भगवद्गीते भवद्वेषिणीम्॥ १ ॥

Om Pārthāya pratibodhitāṁ Bhagavatā Nārāyaṇena svayam
Vyāsena grathitāṁ purāṇamuninā madhyemahābhāratam
advaitāmṛtavarṣiṇīṁ bhagavatīmaṣṭādaśādhyāyinīm
amba tvāmanusandadhāmi Bhagavadgīte bhavadveṣiṇīm 1

ॐ Om पार्थाय to Pārtha (Arjuna) प्रतिबोधिताम् which is taught भगवता नारायणेन by Bhagavān Nārāyaṇa स्वयम् one's own व्यासेन by Vyāsa ग्रथिताम् which is composed पुराणमुनिना by ancient sage मध्येमहाभारतम् in the middle of the Mahābhārata अद्वैतामृतवर्षिणीम् which showers the nectar of non-duality भगवतीम् glorious अष्टादशाध्यायिनीम् which contains eighteen chapters अम्ब O mother त्वाम् you अनुसन्दधामि (I) constantly meditate भगवद्गीते O Bhagavad Gītā भवद्वेषिणीम् which is an antidote to *saṁsāra* terrestrial-entanglement

1. Om. O mother Bhagavad Gītā — by which Pārtha (Arjuna) was enlightened by Lord Nārāyaṇa Himself, which was composed and placed in the middle of the Mahābhārata by the ancient sage Vyāsa, which showers the nectar of non-duality, which is glorious, which contains eighteen chapters, which is an antidote to *saṁsāra* terrestrial-entanglement — I constantly meditate upon Thee.

The first verse is an invocation to the text, Bhagavad Gītā. It starts with Om, the symbol of the supreme God, *Brahman.* Om represents the goal of spiritual Enlightenment.

The invocation is chanted by the guru and disciple. They bow in reverence to the sacred book. Address it as mother Gītā. The Gītā demonstrates the warmth and patience of a mother. Ever ready to comfort and advise erring souls. One may repeatedly take to the wrong ways of life and still approach the Gītā for help.

The rest of the verse contains adjectival clauses glorifying the Gītā:

**By which Pārtha (Arjuna) was enlightened by Lord Nārāyaṇa Himself**

The Bhagavad Gītā is the sermon given by Lord Kṛṣṇa in the battlefield of Kurukṣetra. Kṛṣṇa, being a Self-realised Soul, is acclaimed as the supreme God, Lord Nārāyana Himself. Pārtha is another name of Arjuna.

Arjuna was one of the greatest warriors of his time. Yet, he was overwhelmed with emotion when he saw his revered elders and teachers, relatives and friends assembled in the battlefield. He sunk into utter despondency. Laid down his bow and arrow and refused to fight. Bursting into emotional arguments he wanted to withdraw from the batttlefield. Ending up in total confusion, he surrendered to Kṛṣṇa for guidance. The Lord then enlightened Arjuna with the brilliant philosophy of Vedānta.

**Which was composed and placed in the middle of the Mahābhārata by the ancient sage Vyāsa**

Vyāsa was a celebrated sage of ancient India. He compiled the epic Mahābhārata which contains a hundred thousand verses. The Mahābhārata narrates the rivalry between two royal families, the Pāṇḍavas and the Kauravas. A fratricidal conflict resulting in the Mahābhārata war. The Bhagavad Gītā comprises Lord Kṛṣṇa's sermon. Given to Arjuna in the midst of the battlefield. It contains 701 verses constituting the philosophical essence of the Mahābhārata. The Gītā stands out as a pendant in the necklace of the Mahābhārata.

**Which showers the nectar of non-duality**

The Gītā contains the ancient philosophy of Vedānta. Proclaims the oneness of God and beings. That the supreme Reality is non-dual. Its philosophy is most enchanting. Elevates one to spiritual heights. Renders life most peaceful and blissful. Above all, ushers the seeker to spiritual Enlightenment.

**Which is glorious**

The Gītā is said to be glorious, *bhagavatīm* since it has six attributes known as *bhagas*. They are: *aiśvaryam* absolute might, *dharmaḥ* righteousness, *yaśaḥ* glory, *śrī* beauty, *jñānam* knowledge and *vairāgyaḥ* non-attachment. Both Lord Kṛṣṇa and the Gītā have been conferred with these six glorious attributes.

**Which contains eighteen chapters**

The eighteen chapters of the Gītā may be divided into three sets of six chapters. Together they proclaim the aphorism ***Tat tvam asi*** contained in the celebrated Vedic textbooks. It means **That thou art**. The first set of six chapters explains ***tvam*** **thou.** The next set covers ***Tat*** **That**. **That,** meaning the supreme Reality. The last establishes the congruence of ***Tat*** **That** and ***tvam*** **thou.** You are **That**, the supreme Being.

**Which is an antidote to *saṁsāra* terrestrial-entanglement**

The world is ever in a flux of change. Ill-prepared minds become entangled in the terrestrial fluctuations. Affected and disturbed, they suffer the sorrows thereof. The knowledge of the Gītā teaches one to remain unaffected through these fluctuations. And serves as an antidote to the suffering and sorrow.

The seeker constantly remembers the precepts of the Gītā. His intellect is poised to graft these values in life's activities. Thus, through devotional feeling and intellectual application, the seeker develops reverence for the book. And through reverence he becomes one with it, merges with it.

Verse 2

नमोऽस्तु ते व्यास विशालबुद्धे फुल्लारविन्दायतपत्रनेत्र।
येन त्वया भारततैलपूर्णः प्रज्वालितो ज्ञानमयः प्रदीपः ॥ २ ॥

Namo'stu te Vyāsa viśālabuddhe phullāravindāyatapatranetra
yena tvayā Bhāratatailapūrṇaḥ prajvālito jñānamayaḥ
pradīpaḥ 2

नमः salutation अस्तु be ते to you व्यास O Vyāsa विशालबुद्धे O vast intellect फुल्लारविन्दायतपत्रनेत्र eyes large as petals of full-blown lotus येन by whom त्वया by you भारततैलपूर्णः full of oil of Bhārata प्रज्वालितः well lit ज्ञानमयः replete with knowledge प्रदीपः fine lamp

2. Salutation to you, O Vyāsa: whose intellect was vast, whose eyes were as large as petals of a full-blown lotus, who lit well the fine lamp of all-knowledge, filled with the oil of Bhārata.

Herein the author is worshipped. The Mahabharata epic, in which the Gītā forms an integral part, was written by sage Vyāsa. The seeker adores the great poet-philosopher: Salutations to you O Vyāsa. The rest of the verse contains adjectival clauses glorifying the sage:

**Whose intellect was vast**

The subtlest way of communicating spiritual values is through the intellect. Vyāsa was endowed with a powerful intellect. An intellect that reached out universally. Which broke the barriers of sect, creed or religion.

**Whose eyes were as large as petals of a full-blown lotus**

Communication of knowledge becomes more effective if the master is endowed with an arresting personality. Vyāsa did not lack it. He was handsome, graceful. Comparing his eyes to the petals of a fully blossomed lotus is a poetic expression of his physical handsomeness. Thus the combination of intellectual brilliance and personal magnetism makes Vyāsa an ideal guru.

**Who lit well the fine lamp of all-knowledge, filled with the oil of Bhārata**

The greatness of a guru is not confined to his knowledge and charisma only. It depends on his contribution to the world. Vyāsa is said to have lit the lamp of wisdom. In this metaphor the Gītā serves as a wick. The oil that fuels the lamp is the glory and culture of the Bhārata nation. The light of the Gītā enhances the peace and bliss of humanity.

Verse 3

प्रपन्नपारिजाताय तोत्रवेत्रैकपाणये।
ज्ञानमुद्राय कृष्णाय गीताऽमृतदुहे नमः ॥ ३ ॥

Prapannapārijātāya totravetraikapāṇaye
jñānamudrāya Kṛṣṇāya Gītā'mṛtaduhe namaḥ 3

प्रपन्नपारिजाताय who is *Pārijāta,* tree-of-fulfilment to those who surrender to Him तोत्रवेत्रैकपाणये who is with cane in one hand ज्ञानमुद्राय who is with *jñānamudra,* symbol-of-wisdom कृष्णाय to Kṛṣṇa गीताऽमृतदुहे who has milked the nectar of Gītā नमः salutation

3. Salutation to Kṛṣṇa, who holds a cane in one hand and shows the *jñānamudra* symbol-of-wisdom (with the other),

who is *Pārijāta,* tree-of-fulfilment to those who surrender to Him, who has milked the nectar of Gītā.

The guru, Lord Kṛṣṇa is worshipped in the verse. Who taught the philosophy of the Gītā: Salutations to Kṛṣṇa. Three adjectival clauses describe the guru:

**Who holds a cane in one hand and shows the *jñānamudra* symbol-of-wisdom (with the other).**

Kṛṣṇa was a cowherd boy. In one hand He held the cane used for driving the cattle. With the other hand He displayed the symbol-of-wisdom, *jñānamudra.* This posture conveys a philosophical message.

The word *kṛṣṇa* literally means black, dark. It represents the supreme Self within. Since It is unknown, ignorant to mortals. The Self enlivens the body, mind and intellect to function in the respective fields of activity. But remains neutral, indifferent to the mode of their activities. It supports both evolutionary and devolutionary actions. Kṛṣṇa's posture shows how one could use the Self in one of two ways. To devolve through sensual indulgence. Or evolve by detaching oneself from the body, mind and intellect and gain spiritual Enlightenment.

The cowherd uses the cane to drive the cattle all day to graze on pastureland. By nightfall he herds them home. The cattle are also known to chew the cud. Cattle represent the senses: eyes, ears, nose, tongue and skin. The pastureland, the sense-objects. Colour and form for the eyes, sound for ears, smell for nose, taste for tongue and touch for skin. One spends all day in sensual indulgence. And at the end of the day even relives the pleasures mentally. Like the cattle chewing the cud. Kṛṣṇa showing the cane in one hand, therefore, signifies sensual indulgence, devolutionary activity.

Kṛṣṇa shows the symbol-of-wisdom with the other hand. In the symbol the middle, ring and little fingers are held erect. The forefinger is bent forward to meet the middle of the thumb to form a circle. The three fingers pointing upward represent the body, mind and intellect. The forefinger, the ego. The ego develops because of one's attachment, involvement with the body, mind and intellect. The thumb stands for the supreme Self. When the ego detaches itself from the body, mind and intellect and surrenders to the Self, it gradually merges with Self. Becomes the infinite Reality. The infinite State is indicated by forming the circle. A circle has no beginning, no end. That which has no beginning, no end is said to be infinite. Thus the symbol-of-wisdom signifies the seeker's evolution to spiritual Enlightenment.

Kṛṣṇa, holding the cane in one hand and displaying *jñānamudra* in the other, presents the choice to humanity to use the Self to attain Self-realisation or sink into the lowest of material and sensual life.

**Who is *Pārijāta*, tree-of-fulfilment to those who surrender to Him**

*Parijāta* is described in Hindu mythology as a tree with mystical powers. Whoever stood under the tree and asked for anything, his desire was fulfilled. Kṛṣṇa is said to be *Pārijāta* since he fulfils the desires of his devotees. Whoever surrenders to the Self within overcomes all desires.

**Who has milked the nectar of Gītā**

Being a cowherd, Kṛṣṇa knew the art of milking a cow. Milk is a universal food. Good equally for the young and the old, athletes and invalids, healthy and sick, for one and all. So too the philosophy of the Gītā has a universal application. It removes all stress and strain, doubt and indecision. Ultimately takes one to the state of Enlightenment.

These verses serve both the devotional and the intellectual. To the devotional, Kṛṣṇa is the divine Being blessing His devotees with peace and prosperity. To the intellectual Kṛṣṇa is the Self that serves as the axle around which all activities revolve.

Verse 4

सर्वोपनिषदो गावो दोग्धा गोपालनन्दनः ।
पार्थो वत्सः सुधीर्भोक्ता दुग्धं गीतामृतं महत् ॥ ४ ॥

Sarvopaniṣado gāvo dogdhā gopālanandanaḥ
Pārtho vatsaḥ sudhīrbhoktā dugdhaṁ Gītāmṛtaṁ mahat 4

सर्वोपनिषदः all Upaniṣads गावः cows दोग्धा milker गोपालनन्दनः son of cowherd (Kṛṣṇa) पार्थः Pārtha (Arjuna) वत्सः calf सुधीः pure intellect भोक्ता enjoyer दुग्धम् milk गीतामृतम् nectar of Gītā महत् supreme

4. All the Upaniṣads are cows, the son of the cowherd is the milker, Pārtha the calf, pure intellect the enjoyer and the supreme nectar of Gītā is the milk.

The verse glorifies the text, Bhagavad Gītā. It compares the nectarine philosophy of the Gītā to milk, the Upaniṣads to cows, Kṛṣṇa to the milker, Arjuna to a calf and the pure intellect to those who enjoy drinking the milk.

The cows consume fodder and water to produce wholesome milk. People gain vitality and strength from drinking milk. Though milk is derived from fodder, one cannot gain nourishment directly from the source. The cow has the ability of consuming gross fodder and transforming it into wholesome milk.

Likewise, the great sages of the Upaniṣads have drawn the subtlest philosophy of life from this gross world. The common man cannot do this. Hence he needs the Upaniṣads to do it for him. The cowherd is an expert in drawing milk from the cows. The cowherd, Kṛṣṇa, drew the subtle philosophy of the Gītā from the Upaniṣads for the benefit of the intellectuals.

A cow is known to yield milk more freely in the presence of her calf. Arjuna serves as the calf for Kṛṣṇa to convey the sublime knowledge of the Upaniṣads to intellectual seekers. Ironically, the calf does not benefit as much as the humans who drink the milk. Likewise, Arjuna has not imbibed the philosophy as much as the vast multitude of intellectuals who have benefitted from it.

Verse 5

वसुदेवसुतं देवं कंसचाणूरमर्दनम् ।
देवकीपरमानन्दं कृष्णं वन्दे जगद्गुरुम् ॥ ५ ॥

Vasudevasutaṁ devaṁ Kaṁsacāṇūramardanam
Devakīparamānandaṁ Kṛṣṇaṁ vande jagadgurum 5

वसुदेवसुतम् son of Vasudeva देवम् divine कंसचाणूरमर्दनम् destroyer of Kaṁsa and Cāṇūra देवकीपरमानन्दम् supreme bliss of Devakī कृष्णम् Kṛṣṇa वन्दे (I) salute जगद्गुरुम् universal Guru

5. I salute Kṛṣṇa, the divine son of Vasudeva, destroyer of Kaṁsa and Cāṇūra, the supreme bliss of Devakī, the universal Guru.

Kṛṣṇa is further glorified. This verse also speaks both from the devotional and intellectual angles. The devotee adores Kṛṣṇa as the divine child of father Vasudeva and the supreme bliss of mother Devakī. Who grew up to destroy the tyrants, king Kaṁsa and his chieftain Cāṇūra. Placed

Ugrasena on the throne which the tyrants had usurped. Brought back peace to Mathura. He was the universal Preceptor, *Jagadguru.*

From an intellectual angle the kingdom of Mathura is your individuality. Mathura derivatively means sweetness. Your Self within is all peace and bliss. Kaṁsa and Cāṇūra represent the ego and egocentric attachments and desires. They obscure the Self. Destroy the peace and bliss within. Kṛṣṇa represents the Self. When the individual turns inward and surrenders to the Self within he conquers the ego and egocentric desires. The glory of the Self is restored.

Kṛṣṇa is proclaimed as a *Jagadguru,* universal Preceptor. The teaching refers to the knowledge of the Self. A preceptor can communicate whatever knowledge that he has gained. To the extent that he has unveiled the Self to that extent alone can he communicate. To convey the entire Self he has to unveil the Self completely. Gain spiritual Enlightenment. Thus, the Self alone can convey the Self. Kṛṣṇa, being an Enlightened Soul, is therefore considered a universal Preceptor, *Jagadguru.*

Verse 6

भीष्मद्रोणतटा जयद्रथजला गान्धारनीलोत्पला
शल्यग्राहवती कृपेण वहनी कर्णेन वेलाकुला: ।
अश्वत्थामविकर्णघोरमकरा दुर्योधनावर्तिनी
सोत्तीर्णा खलु पाण्डवै रणनदी कैवर्तक: केशव: ॥ ६ ॥

Bhīṣmadroṇataṭā Jayadrathajalā Gāndhāranīlotpalā
Śalyagrāhavatī Kṛpeṇa vahanī Karṇena velākulāḥ
Aśvatthāmavikarṇaghoramakarā Duryodhanāvartinī
sottīrṇā khalu Pāṇḍavai raṇanadī kaivartakaḥ Keśavaḥ 6

भीष्मद्रोणतटा: Bhīṣma and Droṇa as banks जयद्रथजला Jayadratha as water गान्धारनीलोत्पला king of Gandhāra as blue water-lily शल्यग्राहवती Śalya as shark कृपेणवहनी Kṛpa as current कर्णेनवेलाकुला: Karṇa as high waves अश्वत्थामविकर्णघोरमकरा: Aśvatthāma and Vikarṇa as terrible crocodiles दुर्योधन आवर्तिनी Duryodhana as whirlpool सा that उत्तीर्णा crossed over खलु indeed पाण्डवै: by Pāṇḍavās रणनदी battle-river कैवर्तक: ferryman केशव: Keśava (Kṛṣṇa)

6. The battle-river with Bhīṣma and Droṇa as its banks, Jayadratha as water, with the king of Gandhāra as blue water-lily, with Śalya as shark, Kṛpa as current, Karṇa as breakers, with Aśvatthāma and Vikarṇa as terrible crocodiles, Duryodhana as whirlpool — was indeed crossed over by the Pāṇḍavās with Keśava (Kṛṣṇa) as the ferryman.

The verse describes a terrible river which the Pāṇḍavas crossed over in a boat. The Bhagavad Gītā is compared to the boat. It takes the seeker from the shore of mortality to the shore of Immortality. Kṛṣṇa is the master boatman who ferries the Pāṇḍavas across.

The river is compared to the battle between the royal cousins, Kauravas and Pāṇḍavas. The battle-river is described as being fierce with several obstacles. Bhīṣma and Droṇa are said to be its banks. Bhīṣma was the ancestor of the Kurus, the clan of the royal cousins. And Droṇa was their guru who taught them archery. As stalwarts in the Kaurava army these two determined the course of the battle as the banks do to a river. Jayadratha was the commander of the Kaurava army. His presence was felt everywhere like water in the river. The king of Gandhāra was like the blue water-lily. He was dangerous like the undergrowth of the lily to the passing boat. Śalya was deadly as a shark. Kṛpa taught archery to the Kauravas and Pāṇḍavas before Droṇa did. He was perilous as the current. Karṇa, son of Kuntī, was hazardous as the mighty waves. Droṇa's son, Aśvatthāma and Dhṛtarāṣṭra's son Vikarṇa were menacing as crocodiles. Duryodhana, their leader, was the treacherous whirlpool.

These dreadful obstacles that the Pāṇḍavas encountered symbolise the manifold challenges that one faces in the world. Those who surrender to Kṛṣṇa overcome them with ease. The philosophy of the Gītā helps them to surmount the challenges of life and gain the peace and bliss of the Self within.

Verse 7

पाराशर्यवचस्सरोजममलं गीतार्थगन्धोत्कटं
नानाख्यानककेसरं हरिकथासम्बोधनाबोधितम्।
लोके सज्जनषट्पदैरहरहः पेपीयमानं मुदा
भूयाद् भारतपंकजं कलिमलप्रध्वंसि नः श्रेयसे॥ ७॥

Pārāśaryavacassarojamamalaṁ Gītārthagandhotkaṭaṁ
nānākhyānakakesaraṁ Harikathāsambodhanābodhitam
loke sajjanaṣaṭpadairaharahaḥ pepīyamānaṁ mudā
bhūyād Bhāratapaṅkajaṁ kalimalapradhvaṁsi naḥ śreyase 7

पाराशर्यवचस्सरोजम् born in lake of words of Parāśara's son (Vyāsa) अमलम् spotless गीतार्थगन्धोत्कटम् rich with fragrance of the import of Gītā नानाख्यानककेसरम् many narratives as filaments हरिकथासम्बोधनाबोधितम् instructive in the story of Hari (Kṛṣṇa) लोके in world सज्जनषट्पदैः by the six-footed (bees) of pure people अहरहः day after day पेपीयमानम् always drunk मुदा joyously भूयात् may be भारतपंकजम् the Mahābhārata lotus कलिमलप्रध्वंसि destroyer of the dirt of Kali Eon नः our श्रेयसे for supreme good

7. May the spotless lotus of Mahābhārata — which is born in the lake of the words of Parāśara's son (Vyāsa), which is rich with fragrance of the import of the Gītā, which has many narratives as filaments, which is instructive in the story of Hari (Kṛṣṇa), which is joyously imbibed day after day by bees of the pure intellects in the world, which destroys the impurities of the Iron Age — bestow supreme good on us.

The verse speaks in adoration of the epic Mahābhārata. Compares it to a lotus with adjectival clauses qualifying it:

**Which is born in the lake of the words of Parāśara's son (Vyāsa)**

Parāśara's son was sage Vyāsa. The author of the Mahābhārata. Vyāsa's literary composition was vast, like a lake. And the Mahābhārata, like a lotus.

**Which is rich with the fragrance of the import of the Gītā**

A flower carries a beautiful fragrance. It is compared to the magnificent philosophy of the Gītā. Which the epic Mahābhārata imparts. The Mahābhārata without the Gītā would be like a flower without fragrance.

**Which has many narratives as its filaments**

The lotus has many filaments one within the other. Likewise, the Mahābhārata contains several intertwining narratives. Just as the filaments form the structure of the lotus these instructive narratives build the theme of the Mahābhārata.

**Which is instructive in the story of Hari (Kṛṣṇa)**

Hari is Lord Kṛṣṇa. His joy and cheer, his service and sacrifice, his sense of detachment lend beauty and charm to the epic.

**Which is joyously imbibed day after day by bees of the pure intellects in the world**

The bees go deep into the flower to draw the honey. So do the pure intellects study, reflect upon the Mahābhārata to draw its nectarine philosophy. This is done day after day. It indicates the necessity to be consistent in the study of the scripture.

**Which destroys the impurities of the Iron Age**

The philosophy of the Mahābhārata serves as the antidote to the trial and tribulation, the suffering and sorrow of the time. Those who have imbibed the philosophy emerge purified into a life of peace and bliss.

Verse 8

मूकं करोति वाचालं पङ्गुं लङ्घयते गिरिम्।
यत्कृपा तमहं वन्दे परमानन्दमाधवम्॥ ८॥

Mūkaṁ karoti vācālaṁ paṅguṁ laṅghayate girim
yatkṛpā tamahaṁ vande paramānandamādhavam 8

मूकम् mute करोति makes वाचालम् eloquent पङ्गुम् cripple लङ्घयते enables to cross गिरिम् mountain यत्कृपा whose grace तम् Him अहम् I वन्दे salute परमानन्दमाधवम् most blissful Mādhava (Kṛṣṇa)

8. I salute the most blissful Mādhava (Kṛṣṇa), whose grace renders the 'mute eloquent' and 'cripple scale a mountain'.

Mādhava is yet another name of Kṛṣṇa. The seeker adores Kṛṣṇa as an embodiment of supreme bliss. Who has rendered the 'mute eloquent' and 'cripple scale a mountain'. These achievements indicate the miraculous effect of the life and teaching of Kṛṣṇa. They signify more than what their literal meaning conveys.

Speech is one of the five organs of action. In scriptural literature one of the organs is mentioned to represent them all collectively. Speech would cover the range of human activity. Hence, the mute refers to a dull, inactive person. The knowledge of the Gītā can transform such a person to a bright, dynamic individual.

A cripple is one whose movement is handicapped. A little obstacle could impede his progress in life. The claim here is that he can cross a mountain. A cripple signifies a person with a poor mind and intellect. The mind and intellect together takes one from experience to experience. The Gītā purifies the mind and subtlises the intellect. Perfects the individual to overcome the challenges of this world. And achieve anything in life be it material or spiritual.

Verse 9

यं ब्रह्मावरुणेन्द्ररुद्रमरुतः स्तुन्वन्ति दिव्यैः स्तवैर्वेदैः
साङ्गपदक्रमोपनिषदैः गायन्ति यं सामगाः।
ध्यानावस्थिततद्गतेन मनसा पश्यन्ति यं योगिनो
यस्यान्तं न विदुः सुरासुरगणाः देवाय तस्मै नमः॥ ९॥

Yaṁ Brahmāvaruṇendrarudramarutaḥ stunvanti divyaiḥ
stavairvedaiḥ sāṅgapadakramopaniṣadaiḥ gāyanti yaṁ Sāmagāḥ
dhyānāvasthitatadgatena manasā paśyanti yaṁ yogino
yasyāntaṁ na viduḥ surāsuragaṇāḥ Devāya tasmai namaḥ 9

यम् whom ब्रह्मा Brahmā (creator) वरुण: Varuṇa (sea god) इन्द्र: Indra (lord of heaven) रुद्र: Rudra (god of destruction) मरुत: Maruta (wind god) स्तुन्वन्ति praise दिव्यै: स्तवै: by divine hymns वेदै: by Vedās साङ्गपदक्रमोपनिषदै: by parts, chapters, sections of Upaniṣads गायन्ति sing यम् whom सामगा: singers of Sāma Veda ध्यानावस्थिततद्गतेनमनसा with mind poised in meditation on That पश्यन्ति see यम् whom योगिन: yogis यस्य whose अन्तम् limit न not विदु: know सुरासुरगणा: hosts of gods and demons देवाय to God तस्मै that नम: salutation

9. Salutation to that God whom Brahmā, Varuṇa, Indra, Rudra and Maruta praise with divine hymns, by parts, chapters, sections of Upaniṣads in Vedās, sung by the singers of Sāma Veda, whom the yogis with mind poised in meditation on That perceive, whose limit the gods and demons do not know.

The invocatory prayer ends with an adoration of *Brahman,* the supreme Reality. Here again, there are four adjectival clauses glorifying *Brahman*:

**Whom Brahmā, Varuṇa, Indra, Rudra and Maruta praise with divine hymns**

Brahmā is the creator. Varuṇa, sea god. Indra, the lord of heaven. Rudra, god of destruction. Maruta, wind god. These gods bow down in adoration to *Brahman.* That establishes the supremacy of the Reality.

**By parts, chapters, sections of Upaniṣads in Vedās, sung by the singers of Sāma Vedā**

The Vedic scholars eulogise the Reality in the Upaniṣads of the Vedās. While the Sāma-singers chant its sublime hymns. These evolved souls place the supreme Reality on the highest pedestal.

**Whom the yogis with mind poised in meditation on That perceive**

The yogis are spiritual seers who seek the union with *Brahman.* They render the mind dispassionate and direct it to meditation upon the Reality. The culmination of spiritual practice is the state of single-pointed meditation. Even those highly evolved spiritual practitioners aspire to reach the supreme state of *Brahman.*

**Whose limit the gods and demons do not know**

*Brahman* is the transcendental State of the supreme Reality. It is beyond the cognition of gods and demons. It is not an objective experience. It is a subjective awakening to the supreme State of the Self within.

# II

ॐ सहनाववतु। सह नौ भुनक्तु। सह वीर्यं
करवावहै। तेजस्वि नावधीतमस्तु मा विद्विषावहै।
ॐ शान्तिः शान्तिः शान्तिः।

Om sahanāvavatu. Sahanau bhunaktu. Saha vīryaṁ
karavāvahai. Tejasvi nāvadhītamastu mā vidviṣāvahai.
Om śāntiḥ śāntiḥ śāntiḥ.

ॐ Om सहनौ us both together अवतु (may) protect सह नौ us both together भुनक्तु may cause us to enjoy सह together वीर्यम् vigour करवावहै let us both act तेजस्वि brilliant नौ our अधीतम् study अस्तु may become मा do not विद्विषावहै may dispute with each other
ॐ Om शान्तिः peace शान्तिः peace शान्तिः peace

Om. May (He) protect us both. May (He) cause us to enjoy. May we strive together. May our study become brilliant. May we not become disputatious.

Om Peace Peace Peace

This prayer is chanted both by the *guru* preceptor and the *śiṣya* disciple before starting the study of the scriptures. There are other prayers as well. The chanting of the invocations invocatory prayer helps to calm the mind and tune in the subtle intellect for comprehending the philosophy ingrained in the scriptures.

The human intellect is of two distinct types viz. gross and subtle. When your intellect engages its discriminating faculty in the realm of the terrestrial world it is said to be 'gross'. Gross intellect thinks thoughts pertaining to the world. It discriminates between the pairs of opposites all within the boundary of this world. It could range from the simplest discrimination of a dog between its master and a stranger to the finest discrimination of a scientist in nuclear technology. But all of them are still classified as 'gross' because its field of operation is the terrestrial world. When however your intellect crosses the boundary of the terrestrial world and conceives the possibility of a transcendental Reality, it is called the 'subtle' intellect. No other creature except a human being can posit the transcendental Reality. The subtle intellect is the discriminating faculty which contemplates upon and distinguishes the transcendental Reality from the terrestrial world, discerns the difference between Spirit and matter, between *Ātman* and the world you experience through your material equipments.

The common man engages his gross intellect in the affairs of the world practically all day long. He hardly uses his subtle intellect. It is therefore important to invoke and tune in his subtle intellect for understanding the deeper import of the scriptures. This is achieved by chanting the invocatory prayer. The prayer starts with Om which represents the supreme Reality, the goal of all spiritual pursuits.

The protection sought by the teacher and the taught is only a temporary safeguard against any disturbances that may prevent their study. The prayer is not to be understood as beggary, an outcome of lethargy. Neither the teacher nor the student means to avoid action and begs the Lord to take care of everything. Both of them will be engaged in deep study and reflection. Hence their request to the Lord is to protect them during the period of study from any disturbances. This line conveys their spirit of surrender to the supreme being and their earnestness for study.

In the next two lines they pray for enjoyment and exertion. Spiritual study can bring about results only when the preceptor and the disciple put in their best efforts. They exert their maximum to teach and to learn the knowledge respectively. The teaching and the learning are thoroughly enjoyed by both. Spiritual study ought not to be a drudgery. With the right attitude the study becomes a pleasure.

The next line speaks of the goal of spiritual study. The aim of the spiritual study is the unfolding of the supreme Self. The supreme Self within is at present clouded by *vāsanās*/desires. The study, reflection and the meditation of the knowledge contained in the scriptures help the seeker to exhaust his *vāsanās*/desires and bring out the brilliance of the Self within. This idea is indicated by praying for brilliance.

In the last line the teacher and the taught pray that there be no hatred between them. This appeal is necessary because spiritual knowledge is difficult to administer, difficult to comprehend and that leads to a lot of controversy, arguments and bitterness. The prayer is meant to caution both to avoid such a contingency by being humble and refrain from egoistic and dogmatic assertions.

The three *śāntihs* chanted at the end of the prayer is an appeal to the phenomenal powers to lend peace to their hearts for the pursuit of their study. *Śāntih* means peace. The three *śāntihs* are directed to the three sources of disturbances that destroy mental peace necessary for teaching and learning the contents of the scriptures.

The three sources of disturbances are:

1. *Ādhidaivikam* आधिदैविकम्। (cosmic disturbances)
2. *Ādhibhoutikam* आधिभौतिकम्। (environmental disturbances)
3. *Ādhyātmikam* आध्यात्मिकम्। (inner disturbances)

The first type of disturbance is from the phenomenal powers like lightning, thunder, rain, earthquake etc. Hence the first *śāntih* is chanted loudly. The second type is the environmental disturbance like noise around, animals prowling, insects crawling etc. The second chant is softer than the first to indicate that it is directed to the environmental disturbances. The third type is disturbance springing from one's own body or mind like sickness, worry etc. The last chant is therefore in whispers directed to the inner disturbances.

The invocatory prayer when sincerely and devotedly chanted prepares a proper mental climate for spiritual study and reflection.

# III

ॐ आप्यायन्तु ममाङ्गानि वाक् प्राणश्चक्षुः श्रोत्रमथो
बलमिन्द्रियाणि च सर्वाणि।
सर्वं ब्रह्मौपनिषदं माहं ब्रह्म निराकुर्यां मा मा ब्रह्म निराकरोद-
निराकरणमस्त्वनिराकरणं मेऽस्तु।
तदात्मनि निरते य उपनिषत्सु धर्मास्ते मयि सन्तु ते मयि सन्तु॥
ॐ शान्तिः शान्तिः शान्तिः।

Om āpyāyantu mamāṅgāni vāk
prāṇaścakṣuh śrotramatho
balamindriyāṇi ca sarvāṇi. Sarvaṁ
Brahmaupaniṣadam
māhaṁ Brahma nirākuryāṁ mā
mā Brahma nirākaroda-
nirākaraṇamastvanirākaraṇaṁ
me'stu. Tadātmani
nirate ya Upaniṣatsu dharmāste
mayi santu te mayi santu.
Om śāntiḥ śāntiḥ śāntiḥ

ॐ Om आप्यायन्तु may become strong मम my अङ्गानि limbs वाक् speech प्राणः *prāṇa* vital-air चक्षुः eye श्रोत्रम् ear अथो also बलम् vitality इन्द्रियाणि senses च and सर्वाणि all सर्वम् all ब्रह्म *Brahman* औपनिषदम् of Upaniṣads मा not अहम् I ब्रह्म *Brahman* निराकुर्याम् disown मा me मा not ब्रह्म *Brahman* निराकरोत् may disown अनिराकरणम् no disownment अस्तु let there be निराकरणम् no disownment मे for me अस्तु let there be तदात्मनि to that *Ātman* निरते devoted ये which

उपनिषत्सु in Upaniṣads धर्माः virtues ते those मयि in me सन्तु may be ते those मयि in me सन्तु may be

ॐ Om शान्तिः peace शान्तिः peace शान्तिः peace

May my limbs, speech, *prāṇa* vital-air, eye, ear, and also all my senses grow in strength. All are the *Brahman* of the Upaniṣads. May I not disown *Brahman*. May *Brahman* not disown me. May there be no disownment of *Brahman*. May there be no disownment by *Brahman*. May the virtues of the Upaniṣads repose in me being devoted to that *Ātman*. May they repose in me.

Om Peace Peace Peace

Here is another invocation chanted by the preceptor and the disciple before the study of the Upaniṣads. The chant is meant to appease the mind and render the intellect sharp. This preparation in a student is necessary for him to understand the deep import of the scripture. It also tunes the master's faculties to communicate the sacred knowledge of the Self to the ardent students.

The invocation starts with a prayer to make the limbs strong. To keep the sense organs and the vital-air sheath (life's physiological activities) healthy. By choosing appropriate words the organs of action and perception, and the five physiological activities viz. *prāṇas* are covered. The teacher and the taught understand the importance of keeping all these equipments in good shape for spiritual development. There is no direct relationship between physical and spiritual well-being. Nevertheless, it is important to keep the equipments in perfect condition. It makes it conducive for spiritual development. Just as perfect soil is all-important for good cultivation. The soil does not directly produce the vegetation. Good seeds are the direct cause for good vegetation. Yet the soil is all-important. In the same way the well-being of the body and its limbs, the sense organs and the *prāṇas* are of great importance for self development of a spiritual aspirant.

All are *Brahman* (God). Everything that you perceive, feel and think is *Brahman.* The whole world is nothing but *Brahman* in its essence. This is explained in the Upaniṣads. The Upaniṣads declare that *Brahman* alone exists. Nothing else. That alone is real. Everything that you experience in the world is therefore *Brahman* and *Brahman* alone.

The preceptor and the disciple pray, "May I not disown *Brahman,* may *Brahman* not disown me". The first is an appeal by the intellect while the second is by the mind. The intellect is determined not to deny the *Brahman* because they have both understood that *Brahman* alone is. Nothing else exists. *Brahman* alone has to be realised. The second appeal is devotional. An appeal to God to grant the wishes of the devotee. May God not spurn the request of the devotee to realise God.

The next two lines are a prayer for the masses. May there be no disownment of *Brahman* by anyone. Not only by the teacher and taught in the Upaniṣadic setting but by one and all. *Brahman* is never to be disowned by anybody. The mission in life of entire mankind is to reach *Brahman.* There should be no denial of *Brahman* anywhere. Also a devotional mass appeal. May God also not spurn anybody.

May God grant everyone's prayer. Through these two lines the students of the Upaniṣads demonstrate their selfless nature in including the well-being of all people in their prayer.

The last line of the prayer shows the supreme confidence in the approach to Truth. Both the teacher and student demand as it were the virtues proclaimed in the Upaniṣad for themselves as a right. They richly deserve those virtues as they have worked for them through devotion. '*May they reside in me as I am devoted to the Ātman*' is their plea. As the saying goes: You get what you deserve not what you desire.

As in other invocations, here also the chant ends with three *Śāntihs*. *Śāntih* means peace. May there be peace, peace, peace. It is repeated thrice to indicate that the appeal for peace is directed to three sources of disturbances: *ādhidaivikam* cosmic disturbance, *ādhibhoutikam* the external, objective disturbance and *ādhyātmikam* the internal, subjective disturbance.

# IV

ॐ भद्रं कर्णेभिः श्रुणुयाम देवाः भद्रं पश्येमाक्षभिर्यजत्राः ।
स्थिरैरङ्गैस्तुष्टुवांसस्तनूभिर्व्यशेम देवहितं यदायुः ॥
स्वस्ति न इन्द्रो वृद्धश्रवाः स्वस्ति नः पूषा विश्ववेदाः ।
स्वस्ति नस्ताक्ष्र्यो अरिष्टनेमिः स्वस्तिनो बृहस्पतिर्दधातु ॥
ॐ शान्तिः शान्तिः शान्तिः ।

Om bhadraṁ karṇebhih śruṇuyāma devāḥ
bhadraṁ paśye makṣabhiryajatrāḥ.
sthirairaṅgaistuṣṭuvaṁ-
sastanūbhirvyaśema devahitaṁ yadāyuḥ.
Svasti na Indro vṛddhaśravāḥ svasti naḥ
Pūṣā viśvavedāḥ.
Svasti nastārkṣyo ariṣṭanemiḥ svastino
Bṛhaspatirdadhātu.
Om śāntiḥ śāntiḥ śāntiḥ.

ॐ Om भद्रम् auspicious कर्णेभिः with ears श्रुणुयामः may (we) hear देवाः O gods भद्रम् auspicious पश्येम may (we) behold अक्षभिः with eyes यजत्राः worshipful ones स्थिरैः firm अङ्गैः limbs तुष्टुवांसः singing your praises तनूभिः bodies व्यशेम may obtain देवहितम् allotted by Lord यत् what आयुः span of life स्वस्ति well-being नः for us इन्द्रः Indra वृद्धश्रवाः glorified by ancients स्वस्ति well-being नः for us पूषा Pūṣan, sun विश्ववेदाः all-knowing स्वस्ति well-being नः for us ताक्ष्र्यः Lord of swift motion, Vāyu अरिष्टनेमिः who protects from harm स्वस्ति well-being नः for us बृहस्पतिः Bṛhaspati दधातु may confer
ॐ Om शान्तिः peace शान्तिः peace शान्तिः peace

Om. May we hear the auspicious with our ears O Gods! May we behold the auspicious with our eyes O worshipful ones. May we live God-given span of life with firm limbs and bodies, singing your praises. May the traditionally glorified Indra bless us. May the all-knowing Sun bless us. May Vāyu, protector from harm, bless us. May Bṛhaspati bless us.

Om Peace Peace Peace

This peace invocation starts with Om as in all others. Om represents the supreme Self. It is the ultimate goal of human existence. The *guru* preceptor and the *śiṣya* disciple pray together for that experience.

O gods! O worshipful ones — The prayer is directed to Indra, Pūṣan, Vāyu and Bṛhaspati. These were some of the gods that people worshipped in those days.

The prayer directs the eyes to see auspicious sights. In Upaniṣadic literature one sense organ is used to represent all of them. So the implication is let all the sense organs perceive only that which is auspicious.

The prayer asks for healthy limbs to function perfectly. To sing praises to *Brahman* indicates that the actions perpetrated by the limbs must be of divine nature. The reference to Vāyu and Indra is a subtle indication to the *prāṇas* and the mind respectively. Vāyu is the wind-god which represents the vital-air sheath, *prāṇas.* Indra represents the mind by virtue of his being the king of the sense organs. The Sun and Bṛhaspati refer to the gross and subtle intellects respectively. To the devotional seekers the prayer is merely directed to various gods. The intellectual aspirant finds that all the aspects of his personality — namely the physical body, senses, *prāṇas,* mind and intellect — are covered in the prayer. They are to be in perfect condition for use, in the spiritual pursuit, by both the master and student.

Stimuli from the external world reach you through the organs of perception. Colour and form enter through eyes, sound through ears, smell through nose, taste through tongue and touch through skin. Having entered therein the stimuli react with your mind and intellect. The type of reaction that will set in will depend upon the type of stimulus contacted and the nature of mind and intellect reacting with it. Consequent to the reaction your mind and intellect send out responses back into the world through your organs of action.

The prayer has covered the receipt of stimuli, the reaction within and the responses. All three have to be tuned in perfectly for spiritual Enlightenment.

May we live our allotted span of life — a cry of all spiritual seekers. The Upaniṣad directs the students to live a hundred years. This indicates that a full term of life is necessary and is sought by aspirants for pursuing and reaching the goal of God-realisation.

# V

ॐ शं नो मित्रः शं वरुणः। शं नो भवत्वर्यमा। शं न इन्द्रो बृहस्पतिः।
शं नो विष्णुरुरुक्रमः। नमो ब्रह्मणे। नमस्ते वायो। त्वमेव प्रत्यक्षं ब्रह्मासि।
त्वमेव प्रत्यक्षं ब्रह्मवदिष्यामि। ऋतं वदिष्यामि। सत्यं वदिष्यामिं।
तन्मामवतु। तद्वक्तारमवतु। अवतु माम्। अवतु वक्तारम्।
ॐ शान्तिः शान्तिः शान्तिः।

Om śam no Mitraḥ śam Varuṇaḥ. Śam no
bhavatu Aryamā. Śam na Indro Bṛhaspati.
Śam no Viṣṇururukramaḥ. Namo Brahmaṇe.
Namaste Vāyo. Tvameva pratyaksham̐ Brahmāsi.
Tvameva pratyakṣam̐ Brahma vadiṣyāmi.
Ṛtam̐ vadiṣyāmi. Satyam̐ vadiṣyāmi.
Tanmāmavatu. Tadvaktāramavatu. Avatu
mām̐. Avatu vaktāram.
Om śāntiḥ śāntiḥ śāntiḥ.

ॐ Om शम् propitious नः to us मित्रः Mitra शम् propitious वरुणः Varuṇa शम् propitious नः to us भवतु may be अर्यमा Aryamā शम् propitious नः to us इन्द्रः Indra बृहस्पतिः Bṛhaspati शम् propitious नः to us विष्णुः Viṣṇu उपक्रमः the all-pervading नमः salutations ब्रह्मणे unto *Brahman* नमः salutations ते unto you वायो O Vāyu त्वम् you एव alone प्रत्यक्षम् perceptible ब्रह्म *Brahman* असि are त्वम् you एव alone प्रत्यक्षम् perceptible ब्रह्म *Brahman* वदिष्यामि I shall declare ऋतम् the right वदिष्यामि I shall declare सत्यम् the good वदिष्यामि I shall declare तत् that माम् me अवतु may protect तत् that माम् me अवतु may protect तत् that वक्तारम् the speaker अवतु may protect अवतु may protect माम् me अवतु may protect वक्तारम् the speaker

ॐ Om शान्तिः peace शान्तिः peace शान्तिः peace

May Mitra be propitious to us. May Varuṇa be propitious to us. May Aryamā be propitious to us. May Indra and Bṛhaspati be propitious to us. May the all-pervading Viṣṇu be propitious to us. Salutations to *Brahman.* Salutation to you, Vāyu. You, indeed, are the perceptible *Brahman.* You alone I shall call the perceptible *Brahman.* I shall call you righteousness. I shall call you truth. May that protect me. May that protect the speaker. May He protect me. May He protect the speaker.

Om Peace Peace Peace

Mitra, Varuṇa and Aryamā are three deities *Ādityas* of the heavenly sphere. Mitra is the guardian spirit of the *prāṇa* inhalation and the day. Varuṇa is the deity presiding over the *apāna* exhalation and the night. Aryamā is the presiding deity of the sun and the eyes. These gods are mentioned in the Ṛgveda. The prayer uplifts the devotional attitude of both the preceptor and disciple who chant it before study of the Upaniṣad.

Next, Indra and Bṛhaspati are propitiated. Indra presides over the *devas* gods who represent the senses. So there is a reference to the mind which controls the senses. Bṛhaspati is the god of wisdom. The reference is to the intellect. The all-pervading Viṣṇu, possessed of great strides, identifies himself with feet. This has reference to the bodily movement. Thus, by mentioning all these gods the entire personality of the seeker is covered. All aspects of the seeker's personality are tuned in for the study of the scripture. The physical body, the sense organs, *prāṇa* and *apāna,* mind and intellect have all to be in perfect shape for the pursuit of God-realisation. The personality of the seeker is never neglected in spiritual practices. The seeker has to be fully conscious of the utility of the body and all his equipments and develop them to their optimum capacity for use in the journey to Truth.

*Śam* means well-being. The entire prayer is the invocation for the grace of the gods, of *Brahman* in the unmanifest and manifest form.

Salutation to *Brahman*. *Brahman* is that infinite Reality upon which this pluralistic phenomenon of the world is projected. The goal of life is to realise that supreme Being. To that *Brahman* our humble prostration.

Salutation to you, O Vāyu. Vāyu is considered the perceptible *Brahman*. Vāyu in the form of vital-air, *prāṇa* is directly perceived. It is also called in Vedānta as the *Sūtrātman* meaning the 'evident expression of life'. *Brahman* is the unmanifest Reality while Vāyu represents the manifest's universe.

Ṛtaṁ means righteous. It refers to the meaning of the *śāstras* scriptures. It is to be fully ascertained by the intellect. *Satyam* means the truth. It is to be understood and lived practically. The teacher and taught pray that the knowledge of the scripture be understood and lived by both as a result of the study. Lastly, they ask for protection from any obstacles that may hinder their study and assimilation. This shows their sincerity and deep commitment to the attainment of the highest knowledge.

Om Peace Peace Peace. Om is the symbol of *Brahman*. Peace is invoked to ward off the three obstacles — the *ādhidaivika* heavenly, *ādhibhoutika* external and *ādhyātmika* internal.

# VI

ॐ वाङ् मे मनसि प्रतिष्ठिता,
मनो मे वाचि प्रतिष्ठितमाविरावीर्म एधि।
वेदस्य म आणीस्थः श्रुतं मे मा प्रहासीः।
अनेनाधीतेनाहो रात्रान्सन्दधाम्यृतं वदिष्यामि।
सत्यं वदिष्यामि। तन्मामवतु।
तद्वक्तारमवतु। अवतु मामवतु।
वक्तारमवतु वक्तारम्।
ॐ शान्तिः शान्तिः शान्तिः।

Om vāṅg me manasi pratiṣṭhitā,
mano me vāci pratisṭhitamāvirāvīrma edhi.
Vedasya ma āṇīsthaḥ śrutaṁ me mā prahāsīḥ.
Anenādhītenāho rātransandadhāmyṛtaṁ vadiṣyāmi.
Satyaṁ vadiṣyāmi. Tanmāmavatu.
Tadvaktāramavatu. Avatu Mām avatu
vaktāramavatu vaktāram.
Om śāntiḥ śāntiḥ śāntiḥ

ॐ Om वाङ् speech मे my मनसि in mind प्रतिष्ठिता is rooted मनः mind मे my वाचि in speech प्रतिष्ठितम् is rooted आविरावीर्म एधि *Brahman* reveal Thyself to me वेदस्य of the Veda theme आणीस्थ may (I) master श्रुतम् that (I have) heard मे me मा do not प्रहासीः forsake अनेन by this अधीतेन by studies अहो days रात्रान् nights सन्दधामि continuously live ऋतम् Reality वदिष्यामि think (speak) सत्यम् truth वदिष्यामि will speak तम् that माम् me अवतु protect तत् that वक्तारम् preceptor

अवतु protect अवतु माम् protect me अवतु वक्तारम् protect the preceptor

ॐ Om शान्तिः peace शान्तिः peace शान्तिः peace

May my speech rest on the mind. May my mind rest on speech. O self-effulgent One, reveal Yourself to me. Both (mind and speech) enable me to grasp the Veda. May not my Vedic lore foresake me. I shall join day and night through this study. I shall proclaim the Truth. I shall proclaim the Reality. May That protect me. May That protect the preceptor. Protect me. Protect the preceptor. Protect the preceptor.

Om Peace Peace Peace

The peace invocation is chanted at the commencement as well as the conclusion of the study of Aitareyopaniṣad and other Upaniṣads belonging to the Ṛgveda. 'May my speech rest on the mind. May my mind rest on speech'. Speech, *vāk* is one of the organs of action. In the scriptures one organ is used to represent collectively all the organs. In this case speech is a representative term for all organs of action. *Manaḥ* mind represents thoughts. The prayer starts by asking for a confluence of the speech and mind which means action and thought. The actions of the body must translate the thoughts of the mind. The inner feelings must support the outer expressions in life. The seeker must be an integrated person to be able to tread the path of Truth. If his deeds do not follow his thoughts and his thoughts have no relation to his deeds he remains disintegrated. Such a person falls short of the basic qualification necessary for spiritual unfoldment. The prayer therefore starts with this initial preparation for spiritual study and Enlightenment.

The preparation over, the seeker asks for spiritual Enlightenment. He prays, "O self-effulgent One, O *Brahman,* O God, reveal Your real nature to me. Let my body, mind and intellect help me to grasp the highest Truth. Whatever I have learnt so far let it remain with me. Let not my spiritual knowledge diminish while I am engaged in life's activities". Spiritual wealth has to be carefully preserved as it may corrode when one is involved in the material world.

"I shall join day and night through this study". I shall obliterate the difference between day and night, between the pairs of opposites. One is affected by heat and cold, joy and sorrow, honour and dishonour and numberless other such opposites. In the prayer the seeker earnestly aims to overcome the influence of these opposites. To tide over the opposites is to reach the supreme Reality. The state of Godhood is above the pairs of opposites — *nirdvandva.*

"I shall proclaim the Truth. I shall proclaim the Reality". The seeker is dedicated to the path of Truth. Committed to reach the goal of Self-realisation. The ultimate Reality. For the achievement of this goal the aspirant seeks protection from impediments. "May that Reality protect me. May that protect the preceptor". It is repeated to emphasise the importance of achieving this goal. The guru's protection is sought again and again because he is all-important in this great pilgrimage to Truth.

Om Śāntih Śāntih Śāntih. Om Peace, Peace, Peace. The three invocations are meant to ward off the three kinds of hindrances in the pursuit of *Brahman*. They are the cosmic disturbance, the external disturbance and the internal disturbance.

# VII

ॐ पूर्णमदः पूर्णमिदं पूर्णात् पूर्णमुदच्यते।
पूर्णस्य पूर्णमादाय पूर्णमेवावशिष्यते।
ॐ शान्तिः शान्तिः शान्तिः।

Om pūrṇamadaḥ pūrṇamidaṁ pūrṇāt
pūrṇamudacyate. Pūrṇasya
pūrṇamādāya pūrṇamevāvaśiṣyate.
Om śāntiḥ śāntiḥ śāntiḥ

ॐ Om पूर्णम् whole अदः that पूर्णम् whole इदम् this पूर्णात् from whole पूर्णम् whole उदच्यते comes out पूर्णस्य of whole पूर्णम् whole आदाय having taken पूर्णम् whole एव alone अवशिष्यते remains
ॐ Om शान्तिः peace शान्तिः peace शान्तिः peace

Om. That is whole. This is whole. From the whole, whole emerges. Having drawn out whole from the whole, the whole alone remains.

Om Peace Peace Peace

*Pūrṇam* means 'whole', infinite. *Tat* means 'that'. 'That' refers to *Brahman,* the supreme Reality, the ultimate God. That Reality is whole. It is infinite. It is all-pervading. It pervades the universe which appears before you at present. *Idam* means 'this'. 'This' refers to the visible universe. The universe in its essence is nothing other than the *Brahman.* 'This' too is *Brahman* because there exists nothing other than *Brahman. Brahman* is everything including this universe.

The universe itself appears to be infinite. The universe is made up of time, space and causation. Time is infinite. You can go back in the past into infinity. You can go forward in the future into infinity. Time extends into infinity, both backwards and forwards. So too is space. Space expands into infinite distance on all sides. There is no end to space. Similarly there is no limit to causation. The cause-effect relation can be traced backward and forward *ad infinitum.* So all three — time, space and causation — are infinite. The universe is infinite.

This universe is only a projection upon the supreme *Brahman.* The universe has no status apart from *Brahman.* It is a mere superimposition upon the Reality. It is like the snake superimposed upon the rope. A mere illusory projection. Take away the image of the snake. What remains is the rope. Nothing is lost. The rope remains the same. Similarly discard the universe. What remains is *Brahman.* Take away the infinite universe from the infinite *Brahman,* what remains is still the infinite *Brahman.* Mathematically it is true. Infinite minus infinite equals infinite.

One wonders how that is possible. There is a simple demonstration of this truth. Take a candle light. Let any number of candles be lit from it. The original light is not any less. Millions of lights may be 'taken' from the original light. Still the latter remains the same. So too the infinite *Brahman* remains infinite though infinite universes may be drawn out of it.

That infinite *Brahman* is the goal of perfection for both the master and the student of the Upaniṣad.

Om Peace, Peace, Peace. The three chants are directed to the three types of disturbances viz. the heavenly disturbance far away from you, the worldly disturbance around you and the internal disturbance within you.

# VIII

ॐ प्रातःस्मरामि हृदि संस्फुरदात्मतत्त्वं
सच्चित्सुखं परमहंसगतिं तुरीयम्।
यत् स्वप्नजागरसुषुप्तमवेति नित्यं
तद्ब्रह्म निष्कलमहं न च भूतसंघः॥

Om prātaḥ smarāmi hṛdi saṁsphuradātmatattvam
saccitsukhaṁ paramahaṁsagatiṁ turīyam.
Yat svapnjāgarasuṣuptamaveti nityam
tadbrahma niṣkalamahaṁ na ca bhūtasaṅghaḥ.

प्रातः in the early morning स्मरामि (I) contemplate हृदि in the heart-cave संस्फुरदात्मतत्त्वम् upon that essential Self which is shining सच्चित्सुखम् existence-knowledge-bliss परमहंसगतिम् supreme Goal तुरीयम् fourth यत् that which स्वप्नजागरसुषुप्तम् dream, waking and deep-sleep states अवेति cognises नित्यम् constantly तत् that ब्रह्म *Brahman* निष्कलम् indivisible अहम् I न not च and भूतसङ्घः assemblage of elements.

In the early morning, I contemplate upon that essential Self, shining in the heart-cave, (which is) existence-knowledge-bliss, the supreme Goal, the Fourth, which constantly cognises the waking, dream and deep-sleep states. I am that indivisible *Brahman* and not the assemblage of elements.

The invocatory prayer is a conventional practice of starting a scriptural textbook. This prayer is recited before the study of the Ātmabodha just as the Dhyāna Ślokas are chanted before the Bhagavad Gītā or the Śāntipāṭha before the Upaniṣads.

The prayer directs you to meditate at an early hour of the day upon the Self. It negates the matter equipments and asserts the supreme Self within. The Self alone is your real nature.

The Self is indicated as existing in the cave of your heart. It means that the Self is the core of your personality within the layers of matter which envelop It.

The supreme Self expresses in the gross body as *sat* existence. In the subtle body as *cit* intelligence. In the causal body as *sukham* bliss. Hence, it is referred to as *sat-cit-sukham* existence-knowledge-bliss. It is indicated as the supreme Goal because it is the ultimate experience. There is nothing beyond this experience for mankind to achieve.

The *Ātman* within is also indicated as *Turīyam. Turīyam* means fourth. It signifies the fourth plane of Consciousness. The other three planes of consciousness are the waking, dream and deep-sleep states. *Ātman* is pure Consciousness. It makes one conscious of the realms of the waking, dream and deep-sleep. Hence It is described as the constant Illuminator of these states.

An aspirant is thus led to assert his real personality to be *Ātman,* or *Brahman* as It is also known. *Brahman* is the one homogeneous Reality which does not admit any plurality. Thus asserting his supreme Self he negates this world of plurality which is a mere assemblage of elements.

# Gāyatrī Mantra

Om Bhūr Bhuvaḥ Suvaḥ ॐ भूर्भुवः सुवः
Tat Savitur Vareṇyam तत् सवितुर्वरेण्यम्
Bhargo Devasya Dhīmahi भर्गो देवस्य धीमहि
Dhiyo yo naḥ pracodayāt धियोयोनः प्रचोदयात्

ॐ Om भूः भुवःसुवः Three worlds, the universe तत् That सवितुः Sun वरेण्यम् Most excellent भर्गः Effulgence, radiance, splendour देवस्य Divine, godly धीमहि (We) meditate upon धियः *Buddhis,* intellects यः who नः our प्रचोदयात् unfolds.

Om Bhūr Bhuvaḥ Suvaḥ. We meditate upon the adorable effulgence of the divine Suṇ — May that unfold our intellects.

The one-lettered word symbol ॐ (Om) called *praṇava* represents the supreme Reality beyond the three worlds of the waking, dream and deep sleep. For a study of the detailed significance of the symbol please refer to the chapter on "The Symbol ॐ (Om)" on Page 126.

*Bhūr bhuvaḥ suvaḥ* — are called the *vyāhṛtis.* They represent the three worlds experienced by man. It could be taken in the subjective sense as the waking, dream and deep-sleep states of consciousness or in the objective sense as the higher (heaven), middle (earth) and the lower (hell) worlds. In either case it is meant to represent the whole universe. When man conceives this, he understands his relative insignificance in the vast universe. Man is only an infinitesimal speck in the universe. Yet he asserts his ego and arrogance. This part of the prayer is meant to humble him. He goes through the initial preparation necessary for his mind to lift itself to the realisation of the supreme Self in him.

The prayer is directed to the Sun *(savituḥ)*. In Manusmṛti it is said that the Gāyatrī japa is to be chanted twice in a day at *sandhyā* time. There are two *sandhyās* in a day — dawn and dusk. *Sandhyā* literally means holding together, union, junction. The meeting point of day and night that is twilight in the morning and evening. At this time the Gāyatrī *mantra* is repeated — "We meditate upon the adorable effulgence of the divine Sun. May that unfold our intellects".

The structure of the Gāyatrī has three distinct parts. The first part is the first line consisting of the *praṇava* ॐ and the *mahā vyāhṛtis.* The purpose of the first part is to prepare the seeker's mind for prayer, meditation and Realisation.

The second part consists of the second and third line. It is directed to intensify the seeker's aspiration or determination to reach the goal of Realisation. To develop an intense desire for liberation, called *mumukṣattva* in Sanskrit.

The first two parts involve effort on the part of the *sādhaka,* spiritual seeker while the third part, consisting of the last line, brings about an attitude of self-surrender. The stage of no-effort.

A beautiful metaphor compares these three stages to shooting a target with a bow and arrow. The first stage of preparing the seeker's mind is compared to making the bow by bending a tough flexible rod and tying its ends with a string. The second stage of developing *mumukṣattva* is comparable to positioning the arrow in the bow and pulling the string to its maximum tension. These two aspects of preparation involve effort. The last stage of self-surrender is similar to the release of the arrow when effort has ended. The result of all this is the striking of the target which is the Realisation of the supreme Self.

The Gāyatrī *mantra* is said to be one of the oldest of the divine hymns. It is referred to as the mother of the Vedas. Gāyatrī has a compelling charm of its own to millions of Hindu hearts. The repetition of this mantra with the right understanding of its sacred meaning is believed widely to have the power to dispel all the negative tendencies in the human mind and thereby unfold the supreme Self within.

The greatness of the Gāyatrī is that it has both the power of *mantra* word-symbol and the power of prayer. The pure *mantra* has an inherent effectiveness called *mantra śakti,* that is the power contained in inarticulate or intonational sound. It may or may not have any meaning. But Gāyatrī has both. It has a philosophical meaning. It has the advantage of articulate sound. That is, it has the power of prayer as well. When the power of prayer is combined with the power of *mantra* the seeker is fully equipped with the most effective instrument for the unfoldment of the spiritual potentialities. That is the uniqueness of the Gāyatrī.

Gāyatrī is the *mantra* that is given to the boy at his spiritual initiation called *upanayanam. Upanayanam* is the thread ceremony performed to Hindu boys at a very early age generally between six and eight years. The *guru* preceptor initiates the boy to spiritual study by giving him the sacred Gāyatrī *mantra.* The boy is then considered *dvijaḥ,* which means twice-born. The first birth of the gross personality is when the physical body emerges from the mother's womb. The second birth now is that of the subtle body when the mind and intellect are fully grown and ready to receive the knowledge of the supreme Reality.

The Gāyatrī is chanted both at dawn and dusk facing the sun. The devotee carries a little water in his folded palm and at the end of each chant of the *mantra,* he offers the water to the sun. As the water is offered, the devotee says, "*Asāvādityo Brahma*" which means "This sun is *Brahman* (God)". While saying so he performs the '*Ātma pradakṣiṇā*' by turning himself round from his right side. The Gāyatrī is chanted generally a minimum of ten times during each *sandhyā* but one could chant more according to one's personal capacity.

In the Taittrīya Āraṇyaka there is a story built around this ritual of the daily chanting of the Gāyatrī. It has the typical Vedic mysticism about it. The story describes an island where a tribe of devils called *mandehas* lived. These devils gathered in hordes every morning and approached the sun threatening to destroy him. At that time the water offered by the Gāyatrī-chanters struck them like lightning and they retreated to their island. This happened everyday.

This simple story has a deep philosophical significance. *Manaḥ* means mind and *deha* means body. The devils of *mandeha* therefore signify the desires, passions and cravings of the body and mind. These desires veil the pure Self. They prevent the Divinity from flowing out of your Self. These desires are eradicated by the subtle intellect which is charged with the Gāyatrī *mantra.* Then the inherent brilliance of the Self emerges out of the personality of such a seeker.

The invocation of the sun signifies the invocation of the Self, the *Ātman* within. The *Ātman* is the illuminator of all perceptions, emotions and thoughts just as the sun is the illuminator of all the planets of the solar system. The Gāyatrī *mantra* is an appeal by the seeker to the divine Sun within to emerge out of the cloud of desires and shine forth Its resplendent light.

# PUBLICATIONS BY A. PARTHASARATHY

| BOOKS | Pages |
|---|---|
| Vedanta Treatise | 361 |
| Choice Upanishads | 241 |
| Srimad Bhagavad Gita Volume 1 | 360 |
| Srimad Bhagavad Gita Volume 2 | 265 |
| Srimad Bhagavad Gita Volume 3 | 255 |
| The Symbolism of Hindu Gods & Rituals | 158 |
| Atmabodha (Knowledge of Self) | 138 |
| Select English Poems | 123 |

BOOKLETS (About 40 pages each)

- Are You Stressed
- Increase Productivity
- Value Systems for Positive Living
- Work Ethics for Effective Management
- The Technique of Time Management
- Selections from Vedanta Treatise
- 20 Qualities of a Gnani (Man of Knowledge)
- Dhyana Slokas (Invocation to Bhagavad Gita)
- Bhagavad Gita Booklets

CASSETTES

I Bhagavad Gita : Chapters II-XVIII

II Upanishads:
Kena
Isavasya
Kaivalya

III Guru Purnima:
Fundamental Values of Life
Obstacles in Spiritual Path
How to Select Your Guru

Practise Self-Control
Viveka & Vairagya
Middle Path
Three Yogas
Meditation
Mind & Man
Dilemma of Choice
Elements of True Service
Power of Devotion
Knowledge of the Ultimate
Glory of Renunciation
Use and Abuse of Meditation
Excellence of Enlightenment
The Law of Causation
The 3-C Success

IV Others:
Atmabodha
Bhaja Govindam
Dhyana Slokas
Vedanta Treatise (Talk Book)
Life in Focus
How to Mould Your Children
Overcome Alcoholism Through Vedanta
Harmony in Marriage
Thoughts for the Day
Reduce Stress Through Self-Management
Science of Productivity
Vedanta for Everyday Life
Message for Youth
Personality Chart
Love and Other Mysteries
35 Qualities of a Bhakta (Devotee)
20 Qualities of a Gnani (Man of Knowledge)

**Swami Parthasarathy** is an acclaimed exponent of Vedanta, the ancient philosophy of India. He has a multi-disciplined academic base with post-graduation from London University. He has dedicated his life to the study, research and propagation of Vedanta.

Swamiji's resolve emerged into spiritual avenues as service to humanity:

**Writings**

His books and booklets present the terse scriptural insights in contemporary thought and language. Two books, *Vedanta Treatise* and *The Symbolism of Hindu Gods and Rituals*, have earned best-selling status.

**Vedanta Academy**

Founded in January 1988. The Academy offers continuous three year residential courses for young students from all over the world. And a Diploma in Vedanta on completion.

**Public Discourses**

In English on the Bhagavad Gita and Upanishads have captivated large audiences in India and abroad for over three decades.